RANDOM HOUSE

LARGE PRINT

I'VE BEEN THINKING ...

Maria Shriver

I'VE BEEN THINKING...

Reflections, Prayers, and Meditations
for a Meaningful Life

RANDOM HOUSE
LARGE PRINT

Published in the United States of America by Random House Large Print in association with Viking, an imprint of Penguin Random House LLC, New York.

Cover design by Nayon Cho

The Library of Congress has established a Cataloging-in-Publication record for this title.

ISBN: 978-0-5255-8939-6

www.penguinrandomhouse.com/large-print-format-books

FIRST LARGE PRINT EDITION

Printed in the United States of America

10   9   8   7   6   5

This Large Print edition published in accord with the standards of the N.A.V.H.

For Katherine, Christina, Patrick, and Christopher

I love you all to the moon and back.

Contents

Contents

Contents

Contents

I'VE BEEN
THINKING ...

———————————

Introduction

I've been thinking about how to live a meaningful life for pretty much all of my life.

You see, I grew up in a family where people did really big things. They ran for President. They started programs that changed people's lives. They gave speeches that moved the world. And they never ever gave up trying to make our planet a better place.

Having come from all that, I've thought a lot about how I could create my own space, forge my own path, come up with my own thoughts and beliefs, find my own purpose and mission.

Of course, the quest for a meaningful life is not mine alone. In fact, I believe that every single one of us is here on this earth for a reason. I believe it's our life's work to figure out who we are, what we think, what our gifts are, and how we can make a difference in this world.

Figuring that out takes time and thought. A meaningful life doesn't mean a perfect life. It means making mistakes. It means getting up and trying again and again. It requires strength, faith, hope, and love.

It hasn't always been easy to figure out what I, Maria, believe. Thinking and writing have helped me get there.

This book has evolved from a weekly column I write for my digital newsletter, **The Sunday Paper.** The column is called **I've Been Thinking**—reflections that, I hope, can help us get above the noise of daily life by providing an inspiring path forward.

For this book, I've added to those personal reflections memorable quotations and prayers that have spoken to me at different times in my life.

My hope is that these words will help you chart your path to your own meaningful life. I hope the thoughts expressed here will give you material to meditate on—inspiring you to think, write, and reflect on what makes life meaningful to you.

Because, let's face it: Life is one hell of a rollercoaster ride. At times we feel totally in charge of the journey and love the ride. At other times we feel completely overwhelmed and want to get off. Throughout our lives, we're by turns strong, then weak. We're quite sure we know what we're doing, and then we're utterly and totally lost. We feel elated, and then depressed. We act powerfully, then feel like victims. We're buoyed by courage, then scared out of our wits. We feel a part of a community, and then we feel totally alone. We take pride in our accomplishments, then want to crumble with shame over our mistakes.

I have felt all of this. And what has helped me get through it is my faith, my family, my friends, and my writing.

My writing comes from a place deep in my heart and my mind. Friends and family have often joked that I think too much and I should relax. But for me, thinking and then writing about my life and the world around me helps me to get clear and find peace.

This book is meant to ignite your own reflections and to help you reach your own clarity. My thoughts may not be your thoughts, but they may get you to thinking. Some prayers that settle my soul may not do the same for you, but others may. While I use the word "God" to describe a force larger than myself, I know not everybody does. I'm just sharing with you what has helped me navigate my own life. As they say, "Take what you like and leave the rest."

This book has but one purpose: to get you to think about what constitutes a meaningful life for you. Just you. Because there is only one you, and you have only one life. Here's to making it beautiful and meaningful.

Love always,
Maria

Every morning, I start my day with this version of Saint Teresa's prayer:

May today there be peace within

May you trust God that you are exactly where you are meant to be

May you not forget the infinite possibilities that are born of faith

May you use those gifts that you have received and pass on the love that has been given to you

May you be content knowing that you are a child of God

Let this presence settle into your bones and allow your soul the freedom to sing, dance, praise, and love

It is there for each and every one of us.

—Saint Teresa of Avila

I Am Who I Choose to Become

> "I am not what happened to me. I am what I choose to become."
>
> **—Carl Jung**

There's so much power and aspiration in that statement. Who you become as a person is up to you—up to your imagination, your will, your determination, your choices.

Ever since I was a little girl, I've been fascinated by people's life journeys. I've devoured hundreds of biographies and autobiographies, interviewed countless people from all walks of life—always intrigued by the way people negotiate their ups and the downs, the forks in their road, the hurdles they've faced. In other words, the choices they've made.

And what I've learned is this: No one's life follows a linear path. No one's life is devoid of mistakes, pain, and regret.

What I also know is that no one lives a perfect life. It doesn't matter whether you were born into a famous family or not. No one is immune to some kind of struggle, whether it's mental, emotional, physical, financial, or professional. Everyone has something to work through. And more often than not, that struggle is tough, scary, and lonely. But the good news is that each day gives us the opportunity to choose to begin anew.

So today, start where you are—not where you wish you were, but where you are.

I'm grateful for that realization, because I used to spend so much time beating myself up for choices I'd made that I thought were permanent—and regretting opportunities I was too scared to grab and thought would never come my way again. Or I deluded myself by focusing my attention only on an imagined future, fantasizing there would be a time when everything would magically be as I dream.

But I've learned that living in either the past or the future keeps me up in my head, out of reality, robbing me of the present.

So today, I choose to live in the present. My intention is to authentically be myself as I am today. I try to stay conscious of not judging myself and others. And what I've discovered is that all that time and energy I spent in the past and future I can now spend on my family, my friends, my purpose, and my mission—in other words, my actual life.

One of my favorite sayings is often attributed to Ralph Waldo Emerson: "What lies behind us and what lies before us are tiny matters compared to what lies within us."

So today, start where you are. The past is gone. The future isn't here. This day offers each of us a chance to be the person we want to be. Not the person we wish we had been

yesterday or want to be tomorrow, but the
person we already are.

Dear God, I trust you will meet me right
where I am. Help me to make choices that
are good for me and those I love. Help
me to become the person I'm meant to
be. Help me to say and believe that today,
I am enough and I am worthy. Help me
to know that each day is a gift, and I can
begin anew. Amen.

Seeing the Jewel Inside

"The most fundamental aggression to ourselves, the most fundamental harm we can do to ourselves, is to remain ignorant by not having the courage and the respect to look at ourselves honestly and gently."

—**Pema Chödrön**

Are you looking at the gift wrap or the jewel inside?

No matter who you are, no matter how old you are, the challenge is the same: How do we turn our focus away from the glittering gift wrap we think is us and focus instead on the jewel inside, the jewels we really **are**?

It's hard. I think about the marathon that is life and the endurance it requires. I think about how hard it is to deal with change—to grow old, to see your family change, your friends change, and your own prospects change. All of that sometimes makes it challenging to perceive the beauty within.

The truth is, we all want someone to see the jewel that is inside of us. We all long to be seen as valuable, no matter how old we are. And we work hard trying to get others to recognize our value, our worth, so often giving them the power to decide if we are, in fact, jewels to be cherished.

But that power is actually our own. It's yours. Don't give it away. I know, because I've given it away, and it's challenging to get it back.

I sometimes look in the mirror and wonder who that is staring back at me. But I remind myself that I watched both of my parents age before my eyes, and I loved them no less.

So know this: You are a jewel. Don't get

discouraged when the gift wrap wrinkles or fades. There's something precious inside.

So I've made a decision that now, I'm going to do what I did for my parents: love myself no less as I age. Regard myself not with judgment and criticism, but with kind thoughts, loving thoughts, and then take those thoughts and reflect them out onto others. I'm going to see me—my spirit, my soul, my heart—**now.**

Open your eyes. Look at yourself. See the beauty that is you.

Dear God, I am humbled by the reality that despite my flaws, you love and value me, because I am no better or worse in your sight than anyone else. Teach me how to esteem and love and serve others as you have loved me. Amen.

Working on "Intestinal Fortitude"

> "Failure isn't fatal, but failure to
> change might be."
>
> **—John Wooden**

I've been thinking a lot about what they call "intestinal fortitude." What exactly is it? How do you get it? And how do you cultivate, strengthen, and keep it?

I do know that faith is at the root of fortitude. Strong unwavering faith is built out of small acts along the path of your life. Faith comes directly from your own personal beliefs: knowing who you are and that there's a power greater than you at work in your life—whether you call that power God, Jesus, Buddha, Allah, Adonai, Mary, the Spirit of Lovingkindness, Universal Mind, or something else. That faith, that knowledge, is what helps you come back to yourself, back to your foundation, whenever life shakes you to your core. Now that's fortitude!

People with intestinal fortitude are calm in the storm. They exude a steady, strong, stable energy—the kind of energy you want to be around, follow, and cultivate within yourself. Internal strength with endurance. That means the strength to go on, no matter what.

People who have such fortitude go through life with a strong and unwavering integrity. They don't rage at people or call them names or bully and belittle them. They walk through life with a steadiness that's beyond admirable. In fact, it often seems impossible.

Lately I've been thinking that what we all need right now is a dose of that intestinal fortitude—because I don't know about you, but these days the world feels pretty unsteady to me.

I watch people scream at each other on TV—and not just on reality shows—and I think, "**What the—?!**" So many of us are at war with each other. **What the—?!** Someone running for the highest office in the land calls a female reporter a "bimbo" and people laugh. **What the—?!** Trash-talking is applauded, not reprimanded. **What the—?!** I watch a young reporter and a cameraman with their whole lives in front of them gunned down on live TV, and then I see their assailant tweet it out triumphantly on social media. You know what? Once upon a time, that young reporter could have been me! **What the—?!** What is happening to our culture, our discourse, our politics, our nation?

Then I stop. Enough with the **What the—!** I make a decision. I turn my focus away from all that and instead focus on strengthening my own intestinal fortitude by renewing my own faith—so I can stay strong, stay centered, stay focused on the blessings in life instead of getting sucked into all that hysterical negativity screaming for our attention.

If I cultivate my intestinal fortitude, then when someone calls me or someone I love a "bimbo"—or the next time I hear someone hurl a racial epithet or some other belittling or hateful slur—I will be ready to respond. And I will respond not out of anger or from a position of weakness, but from my newly developed intestinal fortitude. That's where the strength is, where the faith is, where the love is, where the true power lives. It's inside me, in my gut—and in yours, too: the strength to go on, no matter what.

Dear God, help me speak from a place of calm, loving strength. Help me speak with positive intention, not intention to

demean or diminish another. Help me to
find the right words to do that, the right
thoughts, the right tone. Help me to speak
without fear. Help me to speak the truth
with grace and lovingkindness. Amen.

Life Is Yours to Create . . .
and to Re-create

"It's your road and yours alone.
Others may walk it with you, but no
one can walk it for you."

—Rumi

When we're young, we spend a lot of time planning our lives. We look for someone to plan it with. We look for friends to complete it, kids to enhance it, careers to enrich it. We work hard at making all that happen. But life has a way of upending our carefully made plans, and all of a sudden, we can find ourselves having to redesign our lives all over again.

There are examples of that everywhere you look. I have friends whose worlds were pretty much destroyed by addiction, but who then put the drugs down and learned for the first time how to live without destroying themselves and others. No matter how old they are when they stop, they learn the tools to turn everything around. I've also seen women leave abusive marriages and learn that being loved doesn't have to mean being hurt. I've seen kids overcome poverty and be the first in their families to go to college. I've seen people who've lost everything pick themselves up and start over. I've seen people make huge life mistakes, but then recognize it, take responsibility, make amends to those they've hurt, and move on, stronger and better.

In each of these cases, turning their lives around required the courage to face the fear of the unknown. It takes courage to push up against the way it is or the way it has been. It takes courage to push back and be creative with the gift of life. But that's exactly what building a life of our own requires: thinking outside the box, being creative, being flexible, facing the fear of the unknown, stepping into it, and being willing to start over.

Several years ago, I found myself having to re-create my own life. I had to step into the unknown and sit there. It was terrifying. I can't tell you I enjoyed it, but I can say I learned that I could re-imagine, reconstruct, and re-build my life. And every day I continue to do it.

As Steve Jobs pointed out, life can either be limiting, safe, and secure **or** it can be wide open, creative, and sometimes scary.

Your life is yours to create and then recreate. As Mr. Jobs said, "Everything around you that you call life was made up by people who were no smarter than you. And you can change it, you can influence it."

And once you realize that, he said, "you'll never be the same again."

Dear God, you are the God of transformation. Help me to be brave. Help me to trust you and believe that I am here to write my life story in a way that brings glory to you and joy to myself and to others. Amen.

What I Learned About Power from a Community of Nuns

"The moment a woman comes home to herself, the moment she knows that she has become a person of influence, an artist of her life, a sculptor of her universe, a person with rights and responsibilities who is respected and recognized, the resurrection of the world begins."

—Sister Joan Chittister

I traveled to Erie, Pennsylvania, to have a conversation with my friend Sister Joan Chittister about social justice, peace, spirituality, and women.

Sister Joan has been a Benedictine nun for more than sixty years, and in that time, she's written more than fifty books. She speaks out regularly on behalf of women—women in poverty, women in the Church, women who face injustice.

It's always a moving experience for me to visit her community in Erie. It's a peaceful, spiritual place, and this time I experienced the same sense of peace and calm as I did the first time I went.

I arrive late at night. There's a welcoming committee waiting for me at the airport—women who greet me with smiles and hugs. One nun takes the coat off her back and gives it to me, so I won't catch cold.

Everywhere I go in Erie, people are like that, gracious and kind. It actually kind of throws me off. What is it, I wonder? What is it about these nuns and this community that makes it such a haven of lovingkindness?

At the evening event where I've been invited to speak, there are about seventy nuns in the audience of eight hundred. Each one of them is smiling, loving, laughing, smart as all get-out, intellectually curious and sharp. These are women who work in our inner cities, teaching, helping, serving. They don't make any money doing it, largely going unnoticed, rarely mentioned in newspapers or magazines or websites. But, boy, do they seem happy and fulfilled—fulfilled by their vocation, fulfilled by living in a community with one another, fulfilled by service, fulfilled by the simplicity of their lives.

Now I'm not so naive as to think they're without their difficulties. I've read Saint Teresa of Calcutta's diaries, where she reveals her own private struggles with God, her vocation, and her work.

But I bet if any of you went to spend time with this community (and I should point out that visitors are welcome!), going there to write, heal, pray, or just simply be, you'd come out feeling the same as I did: calm, centered, grateful, at home with these servants of peace, and at home in myself.

When we talk about powerful women, we always focus on those in political office, women CEOs on magazine covers, women who star in films and on TV. But I want to focus some attention on women whose power comes from within themselves—not from their clothes or cars, not from their jobs or their spouses. They have none of the trappings that typically make us think people are powerful.

Sister Joan and the others have helped me change my own opinion of power. Power comes from values, from beliefs, from purpose, from within. The women I spent time with this week may not be stepping up to run for President of the United States, but they step up for others every single day. Every single day, they are doing the Lord's work. They speak out for those who are struggling. These women try to make life better for everyone in the world.

I like being around people who are intellectually curious, who are growing, evolving, and interested in their own journey and the life journeys of others. I smile thinking about how much I admire them, respect them, and seek to emulate them. I'm joining their sisterhood of the heart.

Dear God, thank you for blessing me with a wonderful circle of friends who love me and have shared so much of their lives with me. Help me to never take them for granted, but to cherish them more each day. Bless our relationships and help me to bring them into the circle of my new friends who may be blessed and enriched as well. Amen.

The Power of Peace Starts from Within

"If there is light in the soul, there will be beauty in the person. If there is beauty in the person, there will be harmony in the house. If there is harmony in the house, there will be order in the nation. If there is order in the nation, there will be peace in the world."

—Chinese Proverb

I love this old Chinese proverb, because it connects directly what happens in our hearts to what happens in our homes, our country, and the world. What's inside of us is what we put out into our relationships, into our workplace, into our communities, into the culture. If there is rage in us, it affects our families. If there is violence in our hearts and our minds, it will affect others. And so it goes.

Let's start today, and that means starting within ourselves. Think about the importance of having a light in your own soul, as the proverb says. What you think, how you speak, how you parent, how you behave at work—it's all connected.

A friend of mine once suggested her priest come and bless my family's home. So the priest, who had moved to Los Angeles from India by way of the Philippines, came over. He prayed with us. He spoke to us about peace—the peace in our hearts and how that helps us create and live in a peaceful home. He spoke about how it's all connected and how we're all connected.

"Create a peaceful home, a blessed home," he said. "Make that a priority. It doesn't matter how big or how small your home is. Your home should be a place of peace for you and your family. That way, when you go forth from it, you go forth from a place of peace out into the world."

It's so true. We live in rapidly changing and challenging times. We are bombarded with stories of violence. Too many Americans are living in fear, their homes dangerous places in dangerous cities. As a nation, we can do better, but so often we don't.

What can each of us do now that could help us create a more peaceful environment? We can do what this proverb calls upon us to do. We can bless our homes. The home within us, the homes we live in, and the home that is our community.

Peace in the world will take global leaders coming together, but peace in our own hearts can start today, right now. It sounds like a small thing, but it has big implications. Let's bless our hearts and our homes. Let's challenge what is and imagine what can be:

a more peaceful planet for us all. Today I'll meditate on this.

Dear God, I am amazed at the greatness and majesty of all you have created. Thank you for how nature speaks to me of your great power and design. Thank you for the beauty of the flowers and the sunsets and the oceans and the mountains. Thank you for the peace in my own home. Amen.

The Power of Gratitude

"Gratitude is a flower that blooms in noble souls."

—**Pope Francis**

I believe strongly in the power of gratitude. And scientific research backs that up. It shows that making a daily conscious effort to be grateful does in fact make you a happier, more hopeful person.

There are those lucky ones who come by their attitude of gratitude naturally. It seems like they were born happy, optimistic, and grateful. But most of us have to work at having a positive frame of mind. I've found that the best way to get that is to have a daily gratitude practice.

So every morning when I open my eyes,

and before my feet touch the ground, I thank God for the gift of my life. I give thanks for my health, my family, my friends, and for the country I'm blessed to live in. I've found that starting out that way makes for a better day and, in turn, I believe it makes for a better life.

I seek out people who have a gratitude practice. I love talking with them and learning from them. They look at the world through a clear lens. They're more joyful. When adversity arises, they bounce back faster. They know and feel that they have a good thing going. And they do.

The truth is, you can never be grateful enough. So it's worth seeking out people who are like this and asking them how they stay that way: their practices, their principles, and how they put those into action.

The power of gratitude can turn a bad day into a good one. It reboots your spirit.

It makes you look at your life in a different way. Being thankful can make all the difference in your day.

So start your very own daily gratitude practice. Write down what you're grateful for, reflect on what you wrote, and carry the gratitude into your day. It'll make all the difference in the world.

Dear God, thank you for all the times when I am blessed by the kindness of others. You have surrounded me with people who care for me and bless me every day with kind words and actions. Help me to show them the same kindness they have provided. Help me to know how deeply I appreciate them and to know that I treasure them as a gift from you to me. Amen.

The Power of Positive Thinking

"What you're supposed to do when
you don't like a thing is change it.
If you can't change it, change the way
you think about it."

—Maya Angelou

I spend a lot of time thinking. I think about everything: what I read, what I hear, what I see happening around us. I think about what my parents taught me, what my kids say and don't say. You name it, I think about it. And yes, sometimes I overthink it.

Lately I've been trying something new. When a negative thought pops up in my mind, instead of just thinking about it—or more likely dwelling and ruminating on it, even obsessing over it—I think about how I can turn that negative thought into a positive thought. Or as Maya Angelou says, change the way I think about it.

This requires being aware when I'm doing all that deliberating-dwelling-ruminating-obsessing and then making the conscious effort to shift away from it. That means when I notice a thought making negative noise in my head, I stop it ASAP and redirect it into a positive statement, a positive statement with certainty and clarity.

Try it yourself. For example, if you're faced with an impending decision, you may find yourself thinking, "I don't know what to do! I'm confused!" and then get stuck there, paralyzed. But when you become aware that you're doing that to yourself, turn it around to say to yourself, "That's not true. I'm smart. I do know what I'm doing. Yes, I have a decision to make, but I've made a many good decisions in my life, and I'm going to make another one."

Or if you're thinking something like "I'm going to fall apart when my youngest son graduates," (oh, God!)—turn it around. "I'm going to be absolutely fine when my son graduates. I've prepared him well. He's so excited to be moving on, and I myself am excited about this new time in my life." (That actually worked for me.)

The first thought puts you in a place of doubt, the second puts you in a place of power.

Staying stuck up in your head in negativity keeps you out of the reality of your life and robs you of your intuition. Negative thinking gives you a negative mindset and a negative outlook on your life. It also keeps you paralyzed by fear and anxiety. That's what you're doing to yourself with your own thinking.

The mind can be a powerful ally or a formidable opponent. Athletes know this truth very well and are taught mental-strength exercises, because coaches know that mental strength is as important—sometimes more important—than physical strength. Just as you exercise your body, you must also train your mind to work for you and not against you. You need to train for those times when you suffer a setback or a disappointment. You've got to do your reps, over and over and over again.

So do as athletes do after a loss: they reset, refocus, reframe and, yes, reimagine, and get back into training. You must train harder if life knocks you down.

We all need to learn mental strength. I like to think of this as the Power of Rising in our own lives. For most of us, rising is a mental job. We have to visualize ourselves rising—rising above disappointment, rising above failure, rising above a negative mindset.

No matter what your age, no matter what your income, no matter what life has thrown your way, your mind will be your best ally in moving you forward. And the truth is, it's not selfish to spend time learning how to redirect your thoughts. It's crucial if you want to live in your power, in your center, in your certainty.

So this day, this week, this year, remember that. Think about what it would take for you to feel indestructible. Remember Maya Angelou's quote when you read something that tells you to get in shape for spring and summer. Remember that although it's great to have your body in shape, it's just as important to get your mind in shape by practicing changing the way you think about things.

Learn how to rest your mind with meditation—how to ignite it with writing, reading, being inspired by another person's story—how to grow it with brain exercises and learning anything new—how to turn it around, so it works on your behalf. Teach your mind to say positive things to you, about you—about why you're here and how wonderful you are. This may sound silly—and it did to me!—but I've learned it works.

Your mind is your asset. It's going to be with you for your entire lifetime, and it's the best partner you'll ever have. So there's no better time than right now to start making it work for you.

Dear God, so many negative, critical thoughts and lies about myself and my circumstances have made their way into my mind. Help me to learn to silence those voices. Help me speak the truth to lies and negativity and to fill my mind instead with what is good and beautiful about me and around me. Amen.

The Power of the Mind

"The mind is everything. What you think you become."

—Buddha

When I was growing up, my mother was always reminding me not to focus on my looks, but on my mind. She would say to me, "Your looks are gonna go, but your mind? That will carry you through."

Unfortunately, that's not true for everyone.

So right now, my mind is intensely focused on the disease that is robbing millions of people of their minds: Alzheimer's. My own mind has me searching for answers as to why a new brain develops Alzheimer's every sixty-six seconds and why two-thirds of those brains belong to women.

Why are women so disproportionately affected by this disease? So far, no one can tell me why this is happening. In fact, I heard another sobering statistic: It would take forty-three football stadiums to hold all the women in America who currently have Alzheimer's disease. Wrap your own brain around that picture.

And so my mind searches for a cure for Alzheimer's. My mind is also focused on living in a way doctors tell me may help delay its onset—exercising, meditating, sleeping, and eating right. I have four kids, and I want to live to see their kids. I want to be able to remember my kids' names and their children's names, because my own father couldn't.

It's beyond mind-blowing to find yourself sitting across from a parent who has Alzheimer's and who has no idea who you are, or worse, who they themselves are. I've been that child, and I would do anything to spare someone else that experience.

I want to be healthy in my mind and my body, and I don't take my health for granted—neither my physical health nor my mental health. And neither should you.

Dear God, I give thanks for the gift of my mind. It is magnificent, beautiful, and unique. It is mine and mine alone. May I be grateful for it and honor it by taking care of it. Amen.

The Power of Women

"No one can make you feel inferior
without your consent."
—Eleanor Roosevelt

I was raised in a family of men, but I also was raised by a formidable mother to believe in the power of women. I was told that everything my brothers did, I could and should do, too. And so I went out and did it.

But slowly I realized that tackle football wasn't my idea of fun, nor was being held down in water polo until I couldn't breathe. And while it's true I did like going to football and baseball games with my brothers, I soon realized I wasn't paying attention to the same things they were.

My mother always told me, "It's a man's world out there, and you need to be tough to compete," but she also stressed that being a woman was my greatest asset. She spoke often of the power of women and mother-hood and the pivotal role of Mary in the Catholic Church. And she would point to her own mother as the single greatest exam-ple of strength she had ever known.

In spite of all this, growing up I always wanted to be one of the boys, but once I was grown up, I realized my mother was right.

While I was First Lady of California, I was privileged to meet many different types of women whom I more than likely would never have met otherwise, and I was moved and inspired by them all. I produced what grew into the largest women's conference in this country. At our annual gathering, thirty thousand women from all walks of life came together to learn, to grow, to share, to be empowered. It was a life-changing event every year, and it taught me that my mother was correct indeed. I saw female strength, courage, resilience, brilliance, and determination up close. These women taught me that women—when seen and heard and validated—can do anything.

Today I love being a woman. I love the energy I can bring into a space. I love being different from men. I love working from both my femininity and my strength.

The power of women has evolved in my lifetime, and in my children's lifetimes, it will evolve even more.

May we reassure ourselves that being a woman isn't a liability. It's an asset. Like any asset, you must invest in it, care for it, recognize its uniqueness, and nurture it forward.

So, unlike my mother, I don't tell my daughters, Katherine and Christina, it's a man's world. I tell my children it's everyone's world. We all bring something unique to the table. And when we women sit at it, there is no doubt in my mind that it becomes a more compassionate, caring, and collaborative table.

If you're a woman, never doubt that you belong at the table. Never doubt that you bring something to it. And never forget to save a seat for someone else.

Dear God, thank you for the good memories of my youth and the women who helped shape my life. Please bless each of them and enrich them for the way they influenced me. Help me to live their wisdom and strength. Help me continue to embrace your plan for my life and keep moving forward into the life you envision for me. Amen.

The Power of Presence

"Let's not look back in anger, or forward in fear, but around in awareness."

—James Thurber

I'm aware that my family is changing. It's been hard for me to watch Christopher, my youngest son, graduate from high school and get ready to go off to college. Yes, I'm super proud of him and happy he's so excited to be embarking on this next great adventure. But it's also been bittersweet for me. He's the youngest of four, so his departure marks the end of an era in my life.

For years, I've revolved my own life around the lives of my kids, Katherine, Christina, Patrick, and Christopher. My days have been packed with early morning and afternoon carpool pickup times, homework sessions, sit-down dinners, runs to Staples for school supplies. My calendar has been packed with football games, dance recitals, parent-teacher conferences, birthday parties, basketball. My weekends have been joyful, because my children and their friends have so often con-gregated at my home to do homework, play games, laugh, and socialize. I've loved it all.

As this chapter of my life is winding down, I want to be incredibly present for my youngest child's final week of school events. Prom, senior class gatherings, goodbyes to all the parents and kids I've shared so much with. I don't want to miss a thing. I want to take it all in. I want to be present, really present, both for my son and for myself.

Being present in the moment requires focus—at least it does for me. I find myself ruminating about the future or the past so often that it takes a conscious effort to make myself mindful of the present, to focus on the now.

As Christopher's last week of high school unfolded, yes, I was thinking back over how his life has also unfolded—but I promise, I didn't miss a thing that was going on that week. As I watched him go to his senior prom, I could accept with my own eyes and mind that he's no longer the baby boy I held in my arms. Now he's a gorgeous, strapping young man, loved and admired by so many for his heart, his nature, and his amazing character.

So I've been present every step of the way. I know I'll struggle with the emptiness that his leaving will create. I know I'll cry. But I also know that if I'm super present, the memories I create will endure and comfort me far into the future.

Your conscious presence in your own life is powerful. It's a gift to be present—a gift for you and for whomever you share your days with.

This has been Christopher's week. Wish me luck. Oh, and buy stock in Kleenex. I've been going through boxes of it.

Dear God, family is so rewarding. Help us to keep our family first above all the demands in our lives and to create an atmosphere where we can grow in our love for one another. Bring us together as you meant for us to be and help us to enjoy one another and understand one another. May joy and laughter and peace fill our times together. Amen.

The Power of the Pause

"Realize deeply that the present
moment is all you ever have."
—**Eckhart Tolle**

Here you are: sitting, taking a break before you hit the Fast Forward button on your life again. I get that. I'm just like you. I live on Fast Forward, too.

But I do have a wish for you. Before you go out and press that Fast Forward button, I'm hoping—actually I'm praying—that you'll have the courage to first press **Pause**.

That's right: press the **Pause** button. I hope we can all learn about what I call The Power of the Pause.

As everybody else is rushing around like a lunatic out there, I dare you to do the opposite. I dare you to pause. Pausing allows you to take a beat, to take a breath in your life.

I'm asking all of us to learn how to pause—especially now, because while I believe the state of our communication is out of control, and I also believe The Power of the Pause gives us an opportunity to fix it.

We all have the power to change the way we, as a nation, a society, speak to one another. We can change our national discourse for the better—what we read online and in newspapers and magazines, what we see on TV, what we hear on the radio. We have the power to change it.

I'm hoping you'll dare to bring change to our community by pausing and changing the channel in our communication.

Pause—and change it from criticism and fault-finding to understanding and compassion.

Pause—and change it from nay-saying and name-calling to acceptance and appreciation.

Pause—and change it from dissembling and dishonesty to openness and explanation.

Pause—and change it from screaming to speaking.

Edmund Hillary once said, "It is not the mountain we conquer, but ourselves." So let's go out to what I call "The Open Field." Pause—and then go beyond!

PAUSE—and take the time to find out what's important to you and make it your own. Find out what you love, what's real and true to you—so those become the things that most often infuse and inform your work, your home, your life.

PAUSE—before you report or pass along something you "heard" but you don't know is absolutely true, something you haven't corroborated with not just one, but two sources, as I was taught to do as a journalist. And make sure that they're two reliable sources—not just two sources who "heard" what you "heard." A lie isn't true just because more than one person heard it.

So PAUSE—before you put a rumor out there as fact. Just because you read it or saw it on TV or on the web no matter how many times, doesn't mean it's true. Don't just pass on garbage because you want to be first. There's no glory in being first with garbage.

PAUSE—before you hit the Send button and forward a picture that could ruin someone's life or write something nasty on someone's wall because you think it's funny or clever. Believe me, it isn't.

PAUSE—before you make judgments about people's personal or professional decisions.

PAUSE—before you join in disparaging someone's looks or sexual identity or intellectual ability.

PAUSE—before forwarding the untrue and inflammatory tidbits that have made it so difficult for would-be public servants and their families to step up and lead.

Sometimes when we pause, we give ourselves the space to realize we need to hold ourselves back from impulsively acting out on ego to make ourselves feel good or better or bigger or "smarter" or more "in the know." Pausing gives us the power to change direction—and with power comes responsibility.

So remember to pause before you sign on with someone or some organization whose work you already know you don't admire and respect. Who you work for is as important as what you do.

You know, I didn't invent this stop-everything-and-pause idea. Henry David Thoreau went off to Walden Pond. Anne Morrow Lindbergh went to the sea. Buddha, Gandhi, Saint Teresa of Calcutta—the greatest and wisest have often stopped and withdrawn from active lives to journey within themselves. The wisdom they garnered there and shared with us has changed the world.

Pause and feel your strength and your vulnerability. Acknowledge your goodness, and don't be afraid of it. Look at your darkness and work to understand it, so you'll have the power to choose who you'll be in this world.

Women: Look at your toughness **and** your softness. You can and should make room for both in your life. The world needs both.

Men: Find your gentleness and wrap it into your manliness. You, too, can make room for both. The greatest men do.

I pray that you will be able to pause and spend time with yourself to give thanks for the journey that has brought you here. Express your gratitude today to all those who have made your journey possible. Pause and be grateful for all the love you have in your life and all the love you've ever had.

As you head out into The Open Field of life, keep your mind open, keep your heart open. Don't be afraid to be afraid. Courageous people are often afraid. In fact, **that's** why they need courage in the first place!

Have the courage to go beyond your fears. Have the courage to go beyond judgment, to go beyond others' rules and expectations. Have the courage to go beyond shoulda-coulda-woulda.

Live and write your own story and then be brave enough to communicate it authentically. Trust me, someone else will be inspired by it and learn from it.

And finally, remember this: Whenever you're in doubt: **Pause**. Take a moment. Look at your options. Check your intentions. And then? And then take the high road.

> **Dear God,** I need to slow my life down to see, really see, the people in my life. Help me to be so conscious of them that I take the time to look into their eyes and connect with the person who is there right in front of me. Amen.

The Power of Listening

"When people talk listen completely. Most people never listen."

—Ernest Hemingway

Today is a new day. May we all take a moment to pause, take a deep breath, and move forward with the knowledge that this moment is all we have. Recently, I've had more questions than answers about what has been happening in our country. I decided that I wanted to spend the week listening—listening to friends, listening to strangers, listening to myself. And so I did.

I listened to my friend tell me that the guy who cuts his hair is angry that so few people understand his experience as a young black man in the United States of America.

My friend was shocked at what was simmering underneath the beautiful facade of this man he thought he knew so well. I listened to another friend whisper about the loneliness, the anxiety, and the pressure of her experience as the provider and caretaker for a big extended family. I had no idea. I listened to another talk quietly about how hard it is to grow old in a society that only seems to value youth. I listened to another rail about the state of our politics and scream about the lack of leaders and leadership and about everyone's apathy.

I listened, and I'm not even sharing the half of what I heard. If I did, it would take you until next week to finish reading.

Everywhere we look, we're inundated with news and information about how terrible everything is. We're divided and segregated by language, by age, by color, by gender, by politics, by zip codes, by technology, by media, by income levels. And yet simultaneously, we're all seeking connection, all seeking some common experience to share—an experience where we can hear another person say, "I hear you," "I understand," "Me, too," "You are not alone."

I've learned this myself by listening when I'm mothering, when I'm reporting, when I'm working with women and families struggling with Alzheimer's. When I've listened long enough to a person I love or any of the people I've met, I always find commonality. I always come away thinking, "We're so much more alike than we think we are. If only we could let down our facades and share our truth."

In my week of listening, I also listened to myself, and I shared what I learned about me. It's something I don't often do.

I shared this: I, too, often feel disconnected, scared, or anxious. I, too, often feel alone in my life experience. I fully understand that my life experience is nothing like that of the young black man who cuts my friend's hair—nor any black person's life experience, for that matter. I want and need to do a better job at understanding that deep divide. I understand that my life experience is also nothing like a white man's or a Latina's or a transgender person's. I need and want to have a better understanding of what their lives are really like. In fact, my own life experience is unlike anyone else's. And guess what? So is yours.

But what we all share, I believe, is a desire to be understood, to be seen, to matter, to belong. As **ourselves**—not for what family, religion, race, or group we belong to or for whom we may be married to. We all share a common experience in our humanity. We all want someone to listen to us, listen carefully to who we really are, what we feel, what we're scared of.

I know it's hard to pause in our daily

lives, to stop and be quiet and truly listen. I know it's hard to hear other people's pain, frustration, anger, and loneliness without internalizing it ourselves or letting our judgments get the best of us. But when you do listen deeply, you realize that while our experiences are vastly different, our hearts and desires are not.

And it's the same on the larger stage. At this time, in this moment, I believe we all want leaders who bring us together. Not just with words, but with experiences and actions. We want leaders to listen, to be brave enough to share themselves with us, so we can get a glimpse into their own humanity, into their own struggles and fears. That's the beginning of connection and trust.

At this time in our country and our world, what we want and need are leaders to ask us to put our own individual greatness to use. Because we can. We can each step forward and offer our own best selves to the world—in our homes, in our schools, in our communities.

Let's imagine another way. Imagine if we made a commitment to listen with open minds and open hearts to find the common thread. Imagine. We just may begin to hear some answers. And they may not come from a podium or out of the computer. They may just be right inside of you. Listen.

Dear God, I pray I will always have good friends around me and that we will influence, encourage, and inspire one another to be the best we can be. I pray for friends who will speak the truth out of love for me, give me sound counsel when I need it, and be of help in difficult times. Help me to be that kind of friend to them as well. Amen.

The Power of Empathy

"The best and most beautiful things in the world cannot be seen or even touched, but must be felt with the heart."

—Helen Keller

Empathy is a feeling. It's different from sympathy, different from tolerance, even compassion. Empathy is the ability to share someone else's feelings, the ability to understand another person's experiences. In short, the ability to walk in someone else's shoes. That can be hard.

I remember many years ago walking with my young son at an outdoor shopping mall. We saw a woman reading fortunes for five dollars. Her pitch was that she would tell you who you were and what your life would be like by reading coffee grounds from your cup. I'm a sucker for that kind of thing. We stopped.

My son sat down, dipped the cup she gave him into her bowl and turned it upside-down over a saucer, revealing the grounds. He waited.

She looked at the pattern of coffee grounds, then looked at him, and said, "Wow! You're an empath! Do you know what that means?"

He said, "I think I do."

She said, "It means you have an ability to understand other people's lives."

I was amazed, because he does.

She told him, "You're going to help people and heal people in the world with your empathy." And he smiled a big smile. I remember how proud he was to have been told he had that quality.

Some of us, like my son, are born empaths. Others of us learn it from our parents, from our children, our teachers—or from some other patient, loving soul who enters our lives. The good news is we can all develop empathy, and our world needs it now more than ever.

I believe that the vast majority of people are good and want to live in a more caring and compassionate world. The path to that world starts with empathy. And because we're more diverse than ever, more globally connected than ever, empathy is needed more than ever.

But I know there are many who believe that vision is out of reach. They tell me the rampant us-versus-them mentality, the demonizing of people who aren't the same as us—all that will continue to take precedence over any feeling of fellowship we might have with each other.

I strongly disagree. I believe that creating a more caring, compassionate, and peaceful world would begin with understanding the experiences of the Other, with appreciating all of our differences, and accepting that people don't have to be/look/live exactly like we do in order to be worthy.

One of the best ways I've found to understand people whose lives are different from mine is to be of service. Through my work with Alzheimer's, volunteering at Special Olympics and Best Buddies, and in service opportunities at my church—I have felt fulfilled, I have felt connected, and I have felt that I understand other people in ways I couldn't have otherwise.

I've discovered that when someone has had empathy for me and my own life experiences, it softens me and encourages me to give that same gift to another, who may be similarly encouraged, and on and on and on.

So today think about the time you have felt someone's empathy for you—and know that that gift resides within you to give to someone else.

Dear God, please give me the gift of empathy, of understanding another person's life experiences. Help me to listen to those experiences without judgment. Soften my heart, so that I may feel the heart of another. Amen.

The Power of Letting Go

"Some people believe holding on and hanging in there are signs of great strength. However, there are times when it takes much more strength to know when to let go and then do it."

—Ann Landers

I've been thinking a lot lately about letting go—about how easy it is to say and how hard it actually is to do.

It's hard to let go—to let go of things, let go of attachments, let go of beliefs that no longer serve you, let go of old stories you tell yourself, let go of people. To let go of the way things were. And it's especially hard to let go of children.

For me, it's ironic that parenting requires

you to be all in, all there, all the time—giving love unconditionally, being totally present—and then it requires you to let go. Zip! Just like that, you're expected to let go. And be happy about it!

I guess that's the cycle of life. You give your all, and if you do, your children are supposed to feel loved, secure, and independent—independent enough to go off (I almost said "abandon you") and live their own lives. And you, the parent, are supposed to be totally fine with that. You're supposed to wave bye-bye with a big smile on your face and feel like you did good.

What the—?!

Letting go is tough for me. I'm doing it, but I admit that I don't like it. Nope, I don't like it at all. That's my honest feeling.

There was the time I went into Bed Bath & Beyond for a third visit in a week. (I had four kids moving—into dorms, out of dorms, into apartments and out, moving moving moving.) I had been there so many times that the manager greeted me cheerfully with jokes like, "Is this it? Is this the last time, the last one?" I smiled as my eyes welled up with tears. My daughter rolled her own eyes and told me to "just relax!" (FYI, I hate being told to relax.) She told me, "Just be happy for us!" She reminded me daily that this wasn't about me, it was about letting my kids do their own thing. Let go. She said, "This is all going the way it's supposed to!"

But sometimes I don't like things the way they are supposed to be. That's why I've needed an infusion of courage in order to move forward.

So when I watched my youngest child graduate from high school and walk across the stage out into adulthood, I admitted to myself that the time had come for me to let go. I knew I had no choice but to do so. **Let go, Maria**, I said to myself. **Let go.** Ha.

Well, the truth is, I know I can and will do it. I have faith. Faith in myself and in my kids. I know this new era of my life is going to be more unscripted and more wide open. That's both scary and exhilarating. The days will no longer revolve around school schedules. The days will become mine to imagine, mine to create.

That also means no more hiding behind my kids, no more saying "I can't go here," or "I can't do that," because of my parenting chores. I will just have to plain old let go. I have no choice.

Of course, I once read that someone said, "Everything I let go of has claw-marks on it!"

But then again, I'm free now. Okay, okay, I'm ready. Because the truth is, **LET GO** also means **LET'S GO!** (Please remind me that I said that!)

Dear God, letting go is hard for me, because I want to hold on and be in control. That makes me feel safe. Help me to realize that I am safe, even when I let go of the way things are and allow them to unfold in the new ways they're supposed to. Amen.

The Power of Thank You

"If the only prayer you ever say in
your entire life is thank you, it will be
enough."

—Meister Eckhart

I've always been a fan of good old-
fashioned manners. I was raised on
them, and I drilled the same mantras
into my kids:

Always say "Please" and "Thank you."
Stand up when an adult walks into the
room. Hold the door for another person. No
phones at the dinner table. Always introduce
yourself, and if you have friends with you,
introduce them as well. Look people in the
eye when they talk to you. Thank all hosts
and hostesses when you go to a party in their
home. Bring a gift when you go to someone's

house—a candle, some flowers, maybe this book? And always, always write a handwritten thank-you note.

I'm a huge fan of handwritten thank-you notes. In fact, I've never hired anyone to work with me who didn't write a handwritten thank-you after the initial interview. Manners never go out of style, and a thank-you never gets old.

I've been thinking a lot about that lately, the power of "Thank You." Those two small words put together make a huge impact. I'm reminding myself of that today.

The reality is, there are so many people we can all thank on a daily basis. But too often, our busy lives get in our way, and we forget. I know I often rush through my day forgetting to thank the very people who make my day in every way: The people I'm blessed to work with. The people who help me at home. The other parents in my circle who've helped me in so many ways for so many years. My friends who pick up the phone simply to say "Hi!" My brothers and sisters-in-law, cousins, nieces and nephews, and of course my kids. The list goes on and on.

I've noticed in my own life that when someone thanks me for something, it touches me. It makes me smile, it makes me happy. I notice it. I notice every time my son's girlfriend writes me that thank-you note. It always makes a big impression. I notice when my kids' friends thank me for doing something for them or when my daughter thanks me for taking her to a concert by giving me a box of doughnuts! Or when my other daughter sends me information about supplements I should be taking (but I'm not). Or when my younger son asks me about my day or the older one brings me a coffee even though I didn't ask for it. Or when my brothers or friends include me when they go out on the town, whether I'm a party of one or have multiple kids in tow. Seemingly small things can make a big difference: a note, a card, a coffee, a phone call, an invite, a thoughtful email—it all adds up. Thank you.

Expressing gratitude, saying thank you, is so powerful. It means that you see the other person, it means that you noticed who they are and what they did. It says to that person, "I want you to know that you matter to me." It's big. It's a sign of manners, but it's also a sign of care.

So to God, to my family, to my friends: Thank you. Thank you for being there for me. Yesterday, today, and every day.

And a special thank-you to my children for the joy and the love you bring to my life and the opportunity you give me to be your mother.

And P.S.: Don't forget to write those thank-you notes!

Dear God, I thank you. I am so grateful that you encourage me to celebrate my life with the wonderful people you have put in my life. Thank you for the many times you have blessed my life by answering my prayers. May I never forget your amazing goodness. Amen.

The Power of Motherhood

"A mother's love for her child is like nothing else in the world. It knows no law, no pity. It dares all things and crushes down remorselessly all that stands in its path."

—Agatha Christie

Sometimes, I pause, take a deep breath, and reflect on the enormity of motherhood. That's right, the **enormity** of it, because it is the biggest, most powerful, most all-encompassing job on the planet.

I feel so blessed, so humbled, and so honored to be the mother of Katherine, Christina, Patrick, and Christopher.

The truth is, I was scared to become a mother. I was raised by a formidable mother. And I was sure I wouldn't or couldn't measure up to the standards she set. I was afraid I'd mess up, afraid I wouldn't know what to do, afraid I wouldn't be good at it, that I would make all kinds of mistakes.

But I've come to realize that we all mother in our own way, and I've come to trust myself in this job.

I know my children, and I know that in their hearts, they know I love them deeply. They know they are and always have been my priority, my joy, my life's greatest purpose.

They know I've made mistakes. They say that my parenting has changed from the oldest to the youngest. They say I've been inconsistent in the way I've raised the boys as opposed to the girls. The girls say I've been way stricter with them. The boys say I spend too much money on the girls. And some of that's actually true. (Sort of.) But even with my mistakes, I do know they've loved me through all of it.

And they've taught me so much. They've taught me to love gently, to nuture. They've taught me patience, kindness, and acceptance. They reintroduced me to the idea of play and having fun. They've helped me keep my sense of humor and my spirit of adventure. Yes, I've traveled the world with them, but the most valuable trips have been the ones where they've taken me deep into their thoughts, their hopes, their dreams, and their fears.

I give thanks to my mother, who is celebrating in Heaven with her own mother. My mother taught me so much about mothering.

What I've learned on my own is that I didn't need to be afraid of all the things I thought I couldn't do. The most important thing I could do and can do is to love—love openly and love unconditionally. Nothing else really matters. Not the to-do lists. Not all the activities. Not all the classes I organized, not all the trips to the mall, to the parent-teacher conferences, to the beach, to the football field. At the end of the day, it's the time we spend loving one another that I think our kids remember the most. The fun dinners, the Uno games, the walks, the talks. That's what I've learned.

It's the love. Mothering is love.

Dear God, thank you for the gift of being a parent. I know my children are a blessing from you. I ask for your continued guidance, patience, and wisdom, as I seek to support my children on their individual paths. Please guide them as well and take care of them when they face life's inevitable hurdles. Amen.

The Power of Laughter

"One day we will look back on all
this and laugh."
—Quite a few people over the years

There's nothing like laughter to turn your day around.

Do you have people in your life who make you laugh? Can you laugh at yourself? Do you make an effort to make sure laughter is as much a part of your life as work, family, and food?

Life as we know it can be challenging—with worries about career and children and parents and health and finances. Laughter is the best thing I've found to let the air out of any situation that feels heavy.

I'm very lucky, because my kids and their

friends make me laugh all the time. One of my daughters is a genius at sending me funny videos. They lighten and brighten my day, and I keep asking for more. I have one friend who writes the funniest emails. They make me laugh so hard that I've created a special folder for them, so I can read them over and over. I have a few friends I can call on who, no matter the situation, can see something funny in it. Always.

I also have a few favorite films I can turn to that, no matter how many times I watch them, always make me laugh: **Wedding Crashers, Knocked Up, Bridesmaids, Stepbrothers**—just to give you an idea of what makes me laugh.

Laughter is a gift we give ourselves. Make sure you keep including it in your life, no matter how old you get, no matter how much your knees and your back hurt. Laughing at yourself changes how you physically feel.

The power of laughter heals, rejuvenates, re-sets our spirits, and brightens our outlook. Don't let it slip away.

Dear God, thank you for the joy I have in my life. Thank you for the gift of laughter, how it lightens my heart. Help me to be a messenger of joy for others, and help me to laugh at myself. Amen.

The Power of Faith

"Do not go where the path may lead.
Go instead where there is no path
and leave a trail."
—attributed to Ralph Waldo Emerson

That Emerson quote sits on my bulletin board, and every time I see it, I smile.

I smile, because it brings me back to my childhood.

Growing up, I admired my grandmother's constant, fervent, unwavering faith. So one day when I had her alone, I asked her, "Grandma! How can I get your kind of faith?"

She looked at me quizzically with her head tilted sideways—like I'd just posed a crazy question. Then she said, "Well, Maria, you just ask God for it. You just ask God to give you more faith. And he will. That's it!"

Over and over in my life, I've had to come back to my faith and ask God for more of it. More faith in God, more faith that there's a larger purpose in life, more faith that the path I'm going down is the right path for me, more faith in myself.

The truth is, if we want to forge our own path in life, if we want to live a life that's uniquely our own, it takes a lot of faith.

Now to be honest, there have been plenty of times when I've lost faith—wondered where I was going and what I was doing. But thank God, I seem to always find my way back.

I usually find my way back by sitting in silence and asking for guidance. When I do that, I'm calmed, and the words come: "Have faith, Maria. Have faith in God and faith in yourself. You are exactly where you're supposed to be."

I have faith I'm here to leave a trail, so I keep walking.

My grandmother was right: Ask for faith. And if you don't get it the first time, keep asking.

Dear God, I acknowledge that in myself I am weak and vulnerable, but I rejoice that you are on my side and that I am no one's victim. Thank you for being strong in my life. Thank you for letting nothing, no matter how painful or powerful, separate me from your love. That makes me victorious, no matter what. Amen.

The Power of Prayer and Meditation

"Prayer is talking to God. Meditation
is letting God talk to you."

—Yogi Bhajan

I was brought up to pray—to recite prayers about God, about Jesus, about Mary, about life. In my prayers, I also apologized for things I'd said and done. I sought forgiveness for being mean to my brothers, for missing Mass, for stealing candy, and more.

As I grew older, my prayers took on a different tone. I prayed for the health and happiness of my four children. I prayed for my friends. When my mother was sick in the hospital, I prayed for her survival—and then when she was dying, I prayed to God to take her and care for her. When my father was struggling with Alzheimer's, I prayed that God would help both him and us get through it. When my son was in an accident I prayed to God to spare him, and I promised I'd never ever miss Mass again. (I didn't keep that promise, and I've had to pray for forgiveness.) Then when my own life unraveled, I prayed for guidance, for help, for support.

As time marched on, I continued to pray—for faith, for forgiveness, for wisdom. But it's only been much later in my life that I've come to meditation.

Meditation didn't come easily to me. In fact, I was a mess of a student. So a friend gave me a gift of some sessions with a meditation teacher. "This will help," she said.

The teacher sat across from me for three days straight while I fidgeted, got up and down, checked my phone, talked, walked around, even cried. I couldn't get still.

Couldn't sit with myself, with my own thoughts, my own inner-ness and inner mess.

But I did stay with it, because I knew I needed to. I knew I needed to get below the surface. I knew I needed to find the calm. I knew I needed to be able to embrace the quiet, so I could listen to God talk to me, talk within me. So I just plain kept at it, and that made the difference.

Now every day I meditate. I start my day in stillness, and I love it. I pray, I reflect, I meditate. I ask for guidance, and I wait for the answer. I pray, I reflect, I meditate, and then I do it all over again.

I recommend prayer and meditation to anyone who wants not just to tell God what you're thinking and feeling, but also to hear what God is trying to tell you, teach you, and show you. I recommend it to anyone who wants to turn their inner mess into inner peace. Amen.

Dear God, may I spend time with you every day, quieting the cares and concerns that make so much noise in my mind, heart, and spirit, so I can hear your wisdom and feel the love you've given me every day of my life. Amen.

The Power of Forgiveness

"The weak can never forgive. Forgiveness is the attribute of the strong."

—Mahatma Gandhi

This is a big one, and my thinking on it has evolved. So take it from me: if you're struggling with forgiveness, be gentle with yourself, because I've learned that forgiveness is a process, and it takes time.

What is forgiveness? It's letting go of a resentment, giving up feeling harmed or damaged. That doesn't mean the harm or damage didn't happen. It means that you're not going to keep revisiting it over and over again, staying stuck in your resentment of the person who caused the harm. Even if it's you.

I've prayed for help with forgiveness. I've tried to talk myself into it. And often, I've pushed myself to the forgiveness finish line before I was really ready to take the action of actually forgiving, only to find myself right back where I started: resentful and feeling bad.

So to truly get to the place I wanted to be—which was to be a steady, solid, peaceful, forgiving person—I started with myself.

When I found myself berating myself for choices I made, opportunities I missed, people I misjudged, behaviors I condoned, the whole thing—I stopped. "No more." I started being kind to myself. Over and over again.

Once I started easing up on myself in this way, I found myself being able to ease up on others. I realized that what I needed, so did they. If I had made mistakes and deserved to be forgiven, so, too, did they. If I had hurt another and could be forgiven and move on, so, too, could they. If I had been critical and judgmental of someone and could be forgiven, so, too, could they.

In other words, if I could let go of my resentments and judgments of myself, I could and should let go of my resentments and judgments of others and just plain move on, instead of staying stuck. I had to give what I was seeking for myself.

Forgiveness is letting go of the need to feel like a victim. Work on it. You'll lighten your load—the load of negativity you carry around.

Dear God, don't let me be caught in resentment or any other form of fear and hate. If they appear, please turn my thoughts into prayer for my enemy or someone in need.
                    —Father Frank Desiderio, CSP

The Power of Your Story

"You never know how your story
might inspire another.
Share what you wish, save some just
for you, and always remember to keep
adding new chapters as you go along."
                                                    —Maria

I consider myself a storyteller, but I have often struggled with my own narrative. Growing up in a famous family, I sometimes didn't know where the family story stopped and my own began. I'd wonder, "Is this my story? Can I share it, if it involves others who live public lives?"

A few years ago I found myself telling my life story to a friend—how I grew up, how people helped me find my own way, helped me in my journalism career, brought me to the West Coast, toughened me up, made me the person I am today.

Midway through my spiel, my friend stopped me cold and said, "Whoa whoa whoa! You're telling your story all wrong!"

"What? What do you mean?"

"**You** are the hero of your own story. Stop making other people responsible for every twist and turn in your life. **You** made the decisions that got you from Point A to Point B. **You** worked hard. **You** navigated your way to where you are today. Your story is a heroine's journey. Tell it that way!"

I balked and said, "No no no no! I didn't do this, I didn't do that! I didn't have to overcome this or that."

Again my friend stopped me. "Stop devaluing your story! Stop comparing it to others. Own it. Tell it in a way that makes you feel proud! You're a survivor, and you're not done yet!"

These words could very well apply to you,

too. Can you write your story in a way that makes you feel good about yourself? Can you write it in a way that makes you proud of yourself? If you have children, when they learn your story, will they understand how strong you are, all the hurdles you faced, the ways you picked yourself up and kept going?

Think of all the decisions you've made that got you here. Not just the stupid ones (because we all have those), but the smart ones, too—the ones that show that you know what you're doing.

A few years ago, I found myself in a discussion about myself with one of my daughters. She was characterizing me and my choices in a less-than-flattering light. That really pushed my buttons! I pushed back with a fury that surprised both of us.

I amazed myself by what came out of my mouth. I recounted in vivid detail all the decisions I had made in my life that directly contradicted the way she was describing me.

Difficult decisions that required strength, stamina, and courage. My bottom line was that I knew what I was doing, that I had made strong choices, and that no one—not she or anyone else—should ever, ever underestimate me or characterize me as anything but a survivor!

She looked at me and said, "Whoa, okay! Calm down! I got it! I get it!"

So the next time you find yourself telling your story to yourself or to someone else—and giving other people the starring roles—stop! Take credit for the life you've created. And if your kid ever tries to tell you that you're someone you're not, push back!

> **Dear God,** help me to tell my story with compassion for myself. Help me to be gentle with myself for the decisions I have made and will make. And help guide me to make good choices as my story continues to unfold. Amen.

Chasing the Illusion of Perfection

> "Perfection doesn't make you feel perfect. It makes you feel inadequate."
>
> **—Maria**

Perfection is an illusion. It's really important to know that.

There's nobody anywhere who is perfect, and anyone who has tried to nail it has failed. Trust me, trying to nail it is a huge waste of your time and will only make you feel worse about yourself.

We live in a world where everyone is showing off and sharing their so-called "perfect" lives: perfect bodies and eyelashes and clothes and careers and homes and cars and love lives and children. Really? Such "perfection" is always an illusion, and measuring yourself up against an illusion is a guaranteed losing proposition. You have to feel less-than, because who can compete with perfection? Especially when it doesn't exist.

Guess what? Human beings aren't perfect. That's what it means to be human. We're supposed to be imperfect.

Everyone I've talked to whose life looks perfect on the outside will whisper in confidence that they've had times in their lives when they felt like they were just keeping their heads above water. I know I have. After each of my kids was born I beat myself up for not bouncing back physically, as I saw so many women on magazine covers do.

I remember when I was First Lady of California and many people thought I had a perfect life—great family, Kennedy hair, beautiful clothes, high visibility, big impact, making a difference. Perfect picture, right? Well, one day a teacher at my kid's school pulled me aside and said, "I know you are super-busy, Ms. Shriver, but I thought you would want to know that—" and now she whispered, "—your son's shoes have holes in them." Ouch! I felt both humiliated and also like I wanted to tell her to go stick her head where the sun doesn't shine. Truth is, I knew about the shoes, but I also knew they were his favorites and he didn't want to give them up. But still I felt outed by her—the veil ripped off of my own illusion of gotta-be-perfect.

That was more than a decade ago. I have since found relief in letting the perfection illusion go. How did I do it? I simply had to face facts and admit my life isn't perfect. My body isn't magazine-worthy. My photos have to be retouched to look good. Sometimes my life has had holes in it, just like my kid's shoes. IT'S THE TRUTH! I've learned some amazing life lessons in the messiness of my life.

One of those lessons is that I shouldn't deplete my energy and self-worth by chasing perfection—like it's some sort of light at the end of the tunnel or pot of gold at the end of the rainbow, just out of my reach. It's out of my reach, because it doesn't exist!

What exists is your life, the life you are in right at this moment. And focusing on some fantasy out there—thinking you're unworthy unless you achieve it—is a guaranteed recipe for frustration, misery, and self-loathing.

There's no such thing as a perfect life. What we need are meaningful lives. A full and meaningful life requires forgiveness of self for our imperfections—and forgiveness of others for theirs. A meaningful life is filled with victories and mistakes, ups and downs, good and bad, right and wrong, dark and light.

Life isn't a straight shot to the winner's circle. It's more like a labyrinth with twists and turns, and you go around and around. Some twists take you the wrong way, and then you have to start over. Other choices take you in the wrong direction, and you have to start over again. That's what's called "learning"! That's what's called "gaining experience." That's what called "living." For all of us.

Dear God, please help me to let go of trying to be perfect. Help me to realize that I am okay as I am. I was born sacred, and I will always be sacred. Help me to remember that when I stay focused on comparing myself to others—or to some illusion of perfection—I always come up short, and that's not honoring the gift of life you've given me. Help me to remember I am one of your precious children, and I am enough. Amen.

Why Acceptance Is the Path to Finding Peace

"If we have no peace, it is because we have forgotten that we belong to each other."

—Saint Teresa of Calcutta

I love that quote from Saint Teresa, because it speaks to our most basic need to belong. It also speaks to what our world needs so much at this moment: peace.

These days it can feel hard to find peace, when every minute, every day, every year seems to be zooming by so fast.

I, for one, want to slow it all down. I want to slow it down and take a step back from it all, so that I can really think about the pathway to peace.

Over the years, I've thought about how peace is connected to our sense of belonging and acceptance. I've come to learn that once you can accept yourself—once you can accept both the light and the dark that exists in yourself and in all of us—you're on your way to finding peace with yourself and within yourself.

Peace within leads to peace in your home, your community, and your country.

When I was growing up, my father never let us belong to the country club near our home because, the club didn't accept African Americans or Jews. He told us we couldn't belong to a place that didn't accept everyone. That has stuck with me my entire life.

America's story has been a place where people felt they could come and find belonging and acceptance. I'm a descendant of immigrants, and my children's father is a first-generation immigrant.

We all want to belong. We all want to be accepted. Recognizing that we share this desire can help us see our shared humanity.

Saint Teresa is right. We do belong to each other. Once we accept that truth, we'll be on our path to peace.

Dear God, help me accept others the same way you accept me. Empower me to accept people who are different and especially those who often experience rejection and are made to feel unacceptable. I want to love others as you have loved me. Amen.

Why It Takes Courage to Care

"Many see care as soft, but it's anything but. It takes courage to care. It takes passion to stand up for someone or something you believe in and care about."

The quote above is from . . . me! Lately I've been thinking a lot about care—the word, the concept, the act of caring.

I think about all the millions of women and men whose lives are devoted to caregiving—whether it's their profession, their family responsibility, or simply because it's who they are and what they do.

I think about care on a personal level. When I had to have surgery, it made me dependent on the care of others. First and foremost, my children, Katherine, Christina, Patrick, and Christopher, cared for me. Then there were the doctors and nurses whom I didn't even know, but who stepped up to care for me and care **about** me.

All of this got me thinking about what care means to me in the most practical of terms. How do I define care? What do I myself care about personally, professionally, and politically? How do I show that I care? How do I know someone cares about me or will care for me? Can your boss really make you feel cared for? Can a political leader? Should he or she even **have** to care about you?

I think so. I think care is one of the most valuable and important principles for a healthy family and for a healthy community and country.

I think this is a good time for all of us to think about what care means to us. Many see care as soft, but it's anything but. Care is a tough, muscular concept. It takes courage to care. It takes passion to stand up for someone or something you believe in and care about.

We must each balance our own idea of care with the world's often cold and sharp judgments that stop the tenderhearted among us from stepping forward.

I'm dedicated to building a more conscious, caring, compassionate, and connected world, and I'm trying to do that while also not caring too much about what others think about me and how I live my life.

If we want to find our passion and our purpose, we have to care about something deeply, and yet not care about what other people say about what we're doing. Remember, those who judge you don't know you, nor do they care about who you really are.

So care for yourself. Care for others. But

don't care too much what others think or say. Get that right, and you can change the world.

My mother used to say to me, "If you have your health, you have everything." I would add that if you have someone who truly cares for you and about you, then you have something money can never buy. And if you yourself also care for someone—truly, honestly, selflessly—then you have the whole wide world.

Dear God, thank you for caring about me and for me. And thank you for allowing me to feel cared for by others. We have been told, "Blessed are the peacemakers," but may I also remember that "Blessed are the caregivers, too." Remind me not to overlook the simple but powerful act of caring. Let me be aware when people extend their caring to me, and may I extend it to others. Amen.

An Omen from God

"Time is our most precious resource, but very few of us use it as wisely as we could. We rush around so much that sometimes we forget to actually live."

—**Maria**

The subject line of the email was "An Omen from God."

It was from my brother Bobby, who was in Morocco for a board meeting of the organizations ONE and (RED), which he co-founded with Bono—organizations that save lives around the world. Saving lives has, in fact, been my brother's life's work. It has actually been the life's work of all of my brothers—Timothy as chairman of the Special Olympics International, Mark as president of the Save the Children Action Network, and Anthony as the founder and chairman of Best Buddies. But this story is about Bobby.

Bobby has devoted his life to working on behalf of others. That's why an exchange he had with a doorman in Morocco stopped him cold in his tracks.

The doorman, who was trying to grab my impatient and restless brother a cab, turned to him and said, "We have time here. Not like you in America. In America, you have no time, so you do not live."

This really made my brother stop (a huge feat, by the way), and that was the message he was sharing with me in his email. "You're so busy, you leave no time to live. Make your time yours," he wrote to me from halfway around the world.

Now I'm turning around and sharing that with you, too, because I believe it to be deeply true. Time is our most precious resource, but very few of us use it as wisely as we should. We rush through our lives with our eyes on our phones, trying to get through one thing after another. We rush around trying to get somewhere that we think will make us happy. We rush around so much that in the midst of it all, we forget to actually live.

Do you make time to live? Time for yourself? Time for your friends? Time for your family? Or are you too busy?

Many months before I got that email, my brother Timothy had asked me to spend some time with him. "Give me a weekend," he said. "I want time with you." I called him up and said, "Yes, let's," and we did. (I'll tell you all about it later in this book.)

I hope you'll take some time to decide whether you're so busy with everything else in your life that you've forgotten those closest to you—forgotten maybe even yourself.

Which brings me back to my brother

Bobby. Recently he moved away from Los Angeles, where he lived for more than twenty years. He packed up his life and his family and left to settle in another state.

At first, I was angry, because I felt like he was leaving me behind. I know that sounds selfish, but that's exactly how I took it at first. Then I came to realize that what Bobby needed was time. Time away from LA, time for himself and his family, time to breathe, time to recalibrate. Time, perhaps, to savor the life he had skipped over for so long while working so hard on behalf of others. I pray that in his new home he finds the time to live the life he is seeking.

All of which brings me to my favorite poem by my friend Mary Oliver. It's called "The Journey," and in it she reminds us that there's only one life you can save, and that's your own. So start there. If you have time for something else after that, go for it. But make what you do with your time matter.

You have only so much time here on earth.
Make it meaningful.

   As the Moroccan doorman taught Bobby:
Take the time to live.

> **Dear God,** when I read this poem by
> Mary Oliver, I felt like it was an omen
> from you to me. Thank you.

THE JOURNEY

One day you finally knew
what you had to do, and began,
though the voices around you
kept shouting
their bad advice —
though the whole house
began to tremble
and you felt the old tug
at your ankles.
"Mend my life!"

each voice cried.
But you didn't stop.
You knew what you had to do,
though the wind pried
with its stiff fingers
at the very foundations –
though their melancholy
was terrible.
It was already late
enough, and a wild night,
and the road full of fallen
branches and stones.
But little by little,
as you left their voices behind,
the stars began to burn
through the sheets of clouds,
and there was a new voice,
which you slowly
recognized as your own,

that kept you company
as you strode deeper and deeper
into the world,
determined to do
the only thing you could do –
determined to save
the only life you could save.
        —Mary Oliver, from Dream Work

I've Learned to Deserve

"If you look at what you have in life, you'll always have more. If you look at what you don't have in life, you'll never have enough."

—Oprah Winfrey

When I was growing up, my parents never spoke to me about what I "deserved." They spoke to me a lot about what was "expected." They were very clear about that.

They expected me to be tough, hard-working, well-read, and smart. They expected me to help others, especially those struggling on the margins. They sent me to work in impoverished parts of the world, so I would realize I was very lucky and really had nothing to complain about. They expected me to go to church every week, to be honest, to help my brothers, my cousins, my community. They expected me to hold my head up and keep walking forward no matter what.

They expected me to stand up when they walked into the room, something I continued through their dying days. The list of their expectations went on and on. And along the way, their expectations of me slowly became my own.

But over time, another word crept into my life. Slowly at first, even timidly, because for me the word and the concept felt foreign, maybe even embarrassing.

That word was **deserve**. To think you "deserve" something when others have so little felt arrogant and selfish—as in, **Who do you think you are?** I got that message from my parents.

But I've come to understand that there is power in the idea of **deserving**.

What you deserve doesn't necessarily have to do with material possessions. It can have everything to do with how you see yourself and how you want to be treated—by yourself and others.

For example, if you're a hard worker, you deserve to be appreciated and respected by those you work with. That's not asking too much. And if you work a lot, you deserve to rest. My parents wouldn't like me saying that, but it's true. Resting your body and your mind isn't being lazy, it's being smart. You and your body deserve to rest, so you can be healthy, emotionally and physically— and then work some more! (That's the part my parents would like!)

You deserve to be treated kindly by your friends, family, and significant others. As I say to my kids over and over, "Your siblings deserve your respect." And as I say to their friends, "So do I. So stand up when I come into the room, look me in the eye when you talk to me, and don't you dare text at the dinner table!" I realize that if we don't treat ourselves as if we deserve these things, it's hard for others to see that actions like those are important.

So what do you deserve? That's up to you. I can only answer with what I have come to believe I deserve.

I deserve to be happy. Much of that is in my control, but just knowing that I deserve it has helped me be happier. And being treated kindly and respectfully starts with how I treat myself.

I deserve to rest and take breaks. That's why I go to Cape Cod every now and then for a few days. I'm not yet at the place where I can say I deserve a really long vacation, but I'm working toward that "deserve."

I'm no longer embarrassed to admit I deserve these things, too: I deserve to have my boundaries respected. I deserve to live in a safe place. I deserve to love and be loved. I deserve the right to dream again. Yes, I do. Dreams are not just for twentysomethings. Dreams are for all of us at any age. I deserve to grieve in the manner that works for me. If that's longer than others would like, so be it. I deserve to have people around me who tell me the truth, lift me up, want the best for me. I deserve to take time for myself. If that's to read, take a nap, go out to lunch with friends, that's fine.

I deserve to laugh as much as I want.

I deserve to not know. That's right. Until I know, I deserve to be unsure or uncertain of how I feel about something or someone. It's okay. I deserve to express my opinions, and I don't deserve (nor, by the way, does anyone else) to be attacked for what I said, for who I am, for what I believe. I deserve the right to change my beliefs once I've seen they hurt me or hold me down, or when I discover a better way.

The list can go on, and it can also grow and change. In fact, I expect it to. I hope it will. I deserve that.

I write all this in the hope that you will think about what you deserve. I hope you will allow space in your life and your mind to have this conversation with yourself way earlier than I had mine. It's not selfish or arrogant. It's a way to be kind and loving to yourself.

This thing called life is a magical journey. I find it doesn't always make sense. It's filled with uncertainty, joy, struggle, surprises, disappointments, and rewards. It isn't always fair or clean and neat. You deserve to design it the way it works for you and then redesign it if you need to.

That's what I've come to expect. That's what I've learned I deserve.

Now go have a great day. You deserve it!

Dear God, you've given me so many gifts. Help me to know that I deserve them. Help me to know that you love me deeply and that I deserve that love. Amen.

Bring Joy into Your Home

"Find a place inside where there's joy,
and the joy will burn out the pain."
—Joseph Campbell

Thank God there's lots of laughter in my home, because I love to laugh.

My kids are funny, and they bring me tremendous joy, as do their friends.

Yes, I really love my kids' friends. In fact, I have a wall in my home where I hang portraits of all of them who consider this their second home. The wall is full, and if anyone gets out of line, I threaten to take that friend's portrait down. Trust me, that works way better than any "time out" I ever gave.

One thing I learned watching my parents is that they always had young friends, and my brothers' and my friends became their friends. Melding generations gave my parents joy and kept them active and socially engaged.

As my own kids have grown and developed their separate lives—and tried to take their friends with them!—I've had to find other ways to bring joy into my life. This is something I have to work on daily.

I'm blessed with my own friends who make me laugh, and that's helped me realize that keeping my joy on is critical as I get older and some un-funny things start to happen.

And I've also learned that I have to stop doing things that block joy. I have to keep turning off that inner voice of critical self-judgment and shame, stop avoiding living in the present by overly focusing on the future, stop numbing myself with cookies and ice cream.

What also works for me is to be of service. My work in the Alzheimer's community brings me joy. I get joy attending a Bible service with my son. I get joy participating in service opportunities in my church community.

Focusing on finding my joy—like Joseph Campbell says in that quote—helps burn out the old shame and pain I still carry.

So get your joy on. Spark joy in yourself, and before you know it, others will gravitate to you for their own joy shot.

Dear God, help me feel the joy in my own heart. Help me feel the joy that is around me. Help me be a messenger of joy in my family. Help me become a beacon of joy in the lives of others. Amen.

When Life Throws You a Curveball, Do This

"I am ready to come out of the woods and to help shine a light on what's already happening around kitchen tables."

—Hillary Clinton

Those words got me thinking about taking time away from the business and the busyness of modern life to go "into the woods"—either literally or metaphorically—after a loss, be it the loss of a presidential election, a job, a spouse, or some other life-altering event.

Why are so many of us uncomfortable when we see someone step off the treadmill of daily life? Is it because we'd be uncomfortable or too scared to take a break ourselves?

Is it because we can't handle loss ourselves? Is it because we don't know how to grieve?

Life throws all of us curveballs, and it can take time and reflection to figure out how to move forward afterward. In fact, some of the most interesting conversations I've ever had around my kitchen table have been with people who have, for one reason or another, stepped off the predictable path of life to look inward before moving outward. Some were forced off the path they were on. Others responded to a feeling that their lives just weren't working the way they should, so they jumped off themselves. They got off the path and headed off into the woods.

And the fact is, pretty much everyone I've ever spoken to after they "came out of the woods" came out stronger on the inside and more open on the outside.

That made me think about a powerful conversation I had with my father when he was deep in the woods with Alzheimer's. He didn't know my name or his own. He wasn't even talking much anymore. I was sitting with him at the table, trying to engage him about something that was clearly uninteresting to him, when he looked me dead in the eye and said, "You know, you have to go internal if you want to go eternal."

We both got quiet and stared at each other, and I knew that I had just been given some profound advice. In fact, my father said some of the most remarkable things to me while he was living with Alzheimer's.

"Going internal"—pausing, reflecting, meditating—allows us to bring sanity into our daily lives. It makes us better people, better professionals, and better leaders. It's better for our brains and our bodies. It's better for our self-respect. It's better for the creative spirit that lives inside all of us.

I watched my own father struggle after he lost an election, as did others in my family. It takes a long time to make sense of such a personal loss. But history is rich with stories of people—from Thoreau to Mandela to Gandhi to Dorothy Day to Pope Francis—who went away and came back with a story to share.

So after life pitches you that killer curveball, walk into the woods. Then come back out and share your story.

Dear God, when I feel confused and uncertain about the direction I should take or how I should deal with a situation or person, help me to find wise counsel. Please help me listen for your wisdom, and lead me to those through whom you speak, who can wisely discern what is right for me. Amen.

It's Okay—in Fact,
It's Crucial—to Grieve

"Grief can surge back like a rogue
wave, even when the person looks just
fine on the outside."

—Kelly Buckley

Change is in the air. My kids are out
of the house now and on their own
way. Everywhere I look, I see and
feel change. And change often involves grief.

Grief. That five-letter word.

You can grieve the death of a loved one.
A friendship may be lost, and you grieve.
You lose a job, and you grieve. A relationship breaks up, a child leaves home—it's all
loss, it's all change, it can all trigger grief.
And how do you deal with it? There's no

one right way to grieve, and it's important to know that your way is okay.

Why? Because grief is something we all experience, but don't always discuss. It comes at you at different times in all kinds of ways. Millions go through this every day—often away from solace, sensitivity, or support.

I know grief in its many forms. Not just following the deaths of family members and friends, but also in the feelings of loss that come with the inevitable life changes we all endure. In my struggle to sort through the sweeping mix of emotions that come with grief, I've found myself endlessly grateful for the amount of thinking Elisabeth Kübler-Ross put into the subject.

That's because I grew up in a family that experienced lots of tragedy and loss, but no one ever discussed it. They just put their heads down and powered on through. So as a child, and then later on, I moved through these terrible experiences pretty much alone, trying to make sense of the losses without any guidance or framework for how to understand them. Decades later, I realized I was still trying to process what had happened, and I thought to myself that there must be a better way.

Then when my grandmother died, my kids had so many questions. Their questions made me realize that I was just as childlike in my understanding of grief as they were. So I felt a need to address the curiosity we all have about loss in its many forms, including grieving a pet. Thus was born my children's book about grief, **What's Heaven?** People thought this book wouldn't sell, and then it went on to tremendous success—proving just how thirsty our culture is for the conversation about loss and how we cope with it.

Then years later, my mother died. I had always been terrified that if anything ever happened to her, I would never be able to survive. When she passed, I experienced the true depths of grief. But unlike what I saw my relatives do when I was growing up—heads down, powering on through—I now actually felt this tremendous loss, and it brought me to my knees. Then two weeks later, my uncle died—and a year and a half after that, my father died, and my marriage ended. So for several years, I was marinating in grief, and it was an incredibly lonely experience. My world stopped, while everything else continued swirling around me. I felt isolated in my grief.

I found comfort in others who had experienced the death of a loved one or multiple deaths. Each time I came across someone else's story of grief, I felt a little less alone. Every time I wrote about it, I felt I'd taken a step forward. Whenever I shared my feelings of grief with someone else, I felt less isolated. And every time I read about someone else's experiences overcoming grief, I got inspired to believe that I, too, would overcome it one day.

But I also know that some people never get over the loss of a loved one. They just manage their way through it. Even to this day, I can find myself suddenly surprised by tears of grief for an old loss. But I now have the awareness of what it is and the knowledge that I can get through it again. And I do.

Being able to experience grief has made me brave. In opening up to it and allowing myself to really feel it, I grew stronger. But in order to do that, I needed to hear the message that it's okay and, in fact, crucial to feel your grief.

Grieving is real, it's an unavoidable part of the human condition, and we don't need to suppress it in order to survive it.

Dear God, I trust you to help me face the unpredictable challenges and storms in my life. I choose to put my eyes on you and remember that you have promised to be with me, no matter what. I know that courage doesn't come just from confidence in my own strength, but from confidence in you. Thank you for the courage to face whatever lies ahead. Amen.

When Is It Time to Move On?

"Do it well, finish it properly, and move on."

—Eunice Kennedy Shriver

As I watched the many funerals of the men and women who died at the hands of the homophobic shooter at the Pulse nightclub in Orlando and listened to what the victims' family members said about their loved ones, I thought about their grief, their loss, and their trauma. I also thought about how they would move on.

When you're in the midst of grief, it's almost impossible to think about "moving on." In fact, it feels almost disrespectful to think about that. People, even well-intentioned ones, will start saying to the bereaved, "You know, you really should move on. It's the only way to heal. It's the only way forward." They think they're doing you a favor by rushing you out of your grief.

"Moving on."

It's another one of those expressions people toss around that's way harder to do than to say. When a loved one dies, when a chapter closes, when a job ends, when a kid moves away—we're all told to just "move on."

My mother used to say, "Move along, move along, just hurry up and move along." I think that was her way of not dwelling, not getting stuck. I'm sure it was her way of staying one step ahead of all those emotions she tried to keep under control and under wraps—especially grief. I get it.

But I, for one, don't like it when someone tells me to move on. (Or, by the way, when someone tells me to just relax, to just not eat this or that, to just stop worrying.) When someone tells me to move on, inside I'm screaming back, **Hello! I would if I could, but I can't, so stop telling me to!**

Breathe, Maria, breathe.

The truth is, moving on comes with time, and people move at their own pace. Rushing someone to move on isn't healthy, it's not fair, and it's not kind. Very often it's not even possible. So leave them alone!

Take it from me: If you haven't moved on from the loss of someone you love, it's okay. Be gentle with yourself. If you haven't moved on from that job you loved and lost, that's okay too. If you haven't moved on from that fight with your best friend, take your time. It's okay. Because sometimes moving on is exactly the **wrong** thing to do. If you convince yourself to move on before you're ready, you're probably moving **out** of your feelings and **into** denial.

My experience is this: If you don't force it, you **will** eventually move on and you **will** move forward. You **will** find your way. One day, without even realizing it, you'll notice that you feel a little lighter, your thinking will be a little brighter. You'll see your life and the endless possibilities of it in a newer, clearer way. Things will just open up. Light will come in, and you **will** wake up. Without even realizing it, you will have moved on in exactly the right way for you—and at exactly the right time.

Dear God, when I look ahead, the future seems scary and leaves me feeling very vulnerable and insecure. When I don't know what is going to happen, remind me that you know the plans you have for me and that you are directing my steps. I look forward with confidence to your leading me into a bright tomorrow. Amen.

Faith Keepers

> "Sometimes, life is gonna hit you in the head with a brick. Don't lose faith."
>
> **—Steve Jobs**

Birthdays are a great time to reflect on blessings.

Each birthday, I acknowledge I'm blessed to have a new year of life. I'm blessed to have a family that loves me and friends who care for me.

One of my girlfriends refers to my other girlfriends as "faith keepers." It's such a beautiful way to put it, and it's so true. My girlfriends keep the faith for me when I can't find it within myself. And I do it for them. And that's what we all need.

Whether you're embracing a new year of

life or a new challenge, find yourself some faith keepers, because it's hard to move forward without faith.

I move forward with faith in myself, faith in the power of good, and faith that I must be a child of a loving God, because otherwise I wouldn't have that group of loving, caring, funny, honest, strong, and slightly crazy faith keepers in my life.

Blessed are the faith keepers in all our lives and in our world.

Go out and gather your faith keepers. Tell them that's who they are, and acknowledge what they do for you.

My wish is that someday you'll have a chance to sit around a table with all your faith keepers and laugh and talk and share. That's the connection we all need. It's one of the marks of a meaningful life.

Dear God, thank you for populating my life with the wonderful women

who are my faith keepers. I know that
you talk to me through them and love
me through them and teach me through
them and laugh with me through them.
Amen.

What Is Love?

"The most important thing that I know about living is love. Nothing surpasses the benefits received by a human being who makes compassion and love the objective of his or her life. For it is only by compassion and love that anyone fulfills successfully their own life's journey. Nothing equals love."

—Sargent Shriver

I've been thinking about love. It's the stuff of great songs, novels, poetry, and films. Loving and being loved is the greatest gift of this life.

My friend wrote something that struck me. She said that, like many women, she spends a lot of her life searching for the love that's depicted in movies or fairy tales. She said she spends so much energy and effort searching for it that she often misses the love that's all around her in her life every single day.

She didn't realize this until she got cancer and finally let all that love in. She regrets missing out on so much love, because she was too busy looking for it to see it. She said she's grateful for the awareness that cancer has given her.

Every day there is love all around us that many of us miss out on, because we're too busy focusing elsewhere.

I noticed that Valentine's Day is a day when many people who aren't in relationships feel bad. And for those people who are in relationships, they can feel lots of pressure that day to come up with something smart, clever, or expensive to "show" how very much they love their Significant Other on February 14th.

But are chocolates, roses, jewelry, and

big fancy dinners what love is really about? Really?

Those things can certainly be part of the equation, but the kind of love I think everyone needs is the love that's already all around us. It's love that is patient, kind, supportive, gentle, and accepting. It's about caring, listening, and being present. It's about forgiveness and understanding. It's when someone brings you a cup of coffee or orders you an iced tea before you arrive, just because they know you like it. It's your friend sending you an article or a poem she likes. Or someone calling just to check in on you.

I'm not saying I don't like flowers or beautiful dinners, because I do. But like my friend, I've often missed acknowledging and experiencing the gift of love that already surrounds me in my life.

Yes, what the world needs now is more love. But what each of us also needs now is to see and experience the real hardworking love that's already there for us in our lives every single day. We need to see it, feel it, and recognize it for what it is: real love in real life.

Dear God, it's not possible for me to fix myself or heal the wounds of a broken heart, but you can. When I feel crushed by disappointment and have my hopes dashed, you are the mender of my broken heart. As you work this miracle in my heart, I also ask you through your great love to give me the courage to love again. Amen.

Loving Motherhood

"Try to put in the hearts of your children a love for home. Make them long to be with their families. So much sin could be avoided if our people really loved their home."

—Saint Teresa of Calcutta

I love Mother's Day, because I love being a mother. I really, **really** love it. I mean deeply love it.

I love my kids so much, sometimes it overwhelms me. I love hanging out with them, laughing with them, traveling with them, playing games with them. I love having their friends over and watching all their lives unfold before my very eyes.

Yep, I love being a mother. Now, that's funny, because, as I've said, it was something

I had been so scared to do. I was scared I wouldn't get it right, terrified I would make mistakes.

Now I know my kids would say that I have, in fact, made some mistakes. My daughters say I favor the boys, and the boys say I spoil the girls. They would say all kinds of other things that I will not commit to print. But I know one thing for sure: I know they know I love them. They know they are my world.

Every Mother's Day I hope to spend the day just being with them and laughing with them. It's really all I want.

I also think of my own mother. Every day since she died, I've missed her. Often some thought will pop into my head, and I'll turn to go call her, then catch myself by remembering, **Oh yeah, she's no longer here.** Something funny happens or I'll struggle with a decision and think, **I'll ask Mummy**, and then I remember she's gone.

But she lives on in me. Her lessons, her

tips, her takeaways are in me, and I pass them on to my children. For instance: Stay connected with your siblings. Reach out to each of them at least once a week. Life is a marathon, not a sprint. Stay focused on the long road. Be of service. From those to whom much has been given, much is expected.

Motherhood is the most powerful job on earth. Our words, our attitudes, and our actions shape human beings long after we are gone. My mother has been gone several years, and yet her voice, her bearing, her view of the world, are as much alive in me as my own heart. That's made me appreciate the incredible power of motherhood.

And yet, so many of us dismiss the role. We say, "I'm just a mother." Or we mention it second, after we talk about our jobs. We feel we need to supplement our motherhood role with other things we're doing, so we still "matter."

But the fact is, motherhood **is** what matters, and I'm so deeply grateful that I've been given the chance and privilege to experience it.

Every Mother's Day, I pray that each of my children—Katherine, Christina, Patrick, and Christopher—can close their eyes and feel the love that's been showered on them, feel the encouragement, feel my gratitude to them and for them. Happy Mother's Day to all of us—mothers and children alike.

Dear God, help me to always remember that the most important job I have here on earth is being a mother. Help me to honor that role and myself for performing it. Amen.

Talk of Love, Not Hate

"Talk of love, not hate, things to
do—it's getting late.
I've so little time, and I'm only
passing through."
—Dick Blakeslee, "Passing Through"

On this day, I'm choosing to follow those words. We have a choice to talk of love or hate. To give up or to get things done. To find purpose or to throw in the towel. To scream and yell or stop and listen. To reach out or shut down.

There's so much we can all do to move humanity forward. There is so much to do, and we are indeed just passing through. I believe we're meant to make our time matter. Each of us is meant for a distinct purpose, and I believe that purpose is to make our world more caring, more conscious, and, yes, more compassionate.

How can you do that? By seeing yourself as someone whose light is what the world is looking for. By seeing yourself as what I call "an architect of change." By seeing yourself as someone who can move humanity forward. By seeing yourself as an instrument of peace.

So, if you're feeling down, confused, or shaken, read the Prayer of Saint Francis. If you're feeling elated, vindicated, or boastful, read the Prayer of Saint Francis. It's withstood the test of time, because it works.

Prayer of Saint Francis

Lord, make me an instrument of your peace:
where there is hatred, let me sow love;
where there is injury, pardon;
where there is doubt, faith;

where there is despair, hope;
where there is darkness, light;
where there is sadness, joy.

O divine Master, grant that I may not
so much seek
to be consoled as to console,
to be understood as to understand,
to be loved as to love.
For it is in giving that we receive,
it is in pardoning that we are
pardoned,
and it is in dying that we are born to
eternal life.
Amen.

We're in Need of a Social Kindness Movement

"Kindness is the language that the
deaf can hear and the blind can see."
—attributed to Mark Twain

My daughter Christina has moved to New York. She left home when she went to college, but then came back again to reconnect and figure out what kind of work she wanted to do. Her passion has always been art and design, so she applied for her master's in business and design in New York, packed her bags, and left once again.

It feels different this time. In my gut, I know she's on her way for good.

I'm happy for her, but as I sit to do my morning meditation, my eyes well with tears, and I feel sad, really sad. You could say—and friends do say—"Snap out of it, and be happy for her!" I am, I am. But I still feel really emotional.

Life is predictable—and yet oh, so unpredictable. We feel blessed one minute and lonely the next. Our lives can feel so full and then so empty. One minute we're laughing, our houses are full, and the next day they can be quiet and desolate.

So goes life. And you never know about someone else's life. It may look easy to you on the outside, but it can be dark and lonely for them on the inside.

I know many, many people understand this. I posted a quote attributed to Plato on social media—"Be kind, for everyone you meet is fighting a hard battle." The quote struck a profound chord, because it was shared almost a million times in just a few days.

We all want to be treated with kindness, because we're all struggling in some way, shape, or form. I had to learn this as an adult, because growing up in a large, competitive, and tough Irish Catholic family, I used to confuse kindness with weakness. When I grew up, I learned differently. I now understand that kindness doesn't mean weakness. You have to be really strong to be kind.

I'm not saying it's easy. But you do have to be strong and patient to be kind. You have to really be mindful and do it.

A person may look "happy on the outside," but who knows what's happening on the inside? Her kid may have just left home, and she's sad. Her mother may be sick. Her home may be in disarray. The list goes on and on.

So let's start a social kindness movement this very moment. Think how kindness makes **you** feel, then move out into the world from there. If we really are the strongest nation on earth, then who better than us to lead a kindness revolution?

And if you see my girl on the streets of the Big Apple, please be kind to her.

Dear God, thank you for the kindness, mercy, and generosity you show me every day, and I ask you to help me to see those around me in the same way—as people who are loved and treasured. Please make my heart as tender as yours, so that I may actively reach out and show kindness and generosity to all the people in my life today. Amen.

Go Back to Move Forward

"Family means no one gets left
behind, or forgotten."
—**Lilo, in** Lilo and Stitch

I make my annual pilgrimage back to Cape Cod in the summers. I used to say that I was going there to see my parents, but now they're both gone. So why do I still go? And should I keep going? It's a question I ask myself a lot. But on the flight back home to California, I realize deep in my heart why I go and why I'm so happy that I still can.

I go to keep my connection with my family strong. I go so that my kids will know their cousins and understand the value of family. I go so that they'll understand that you can have great fun just playing ping-pong or making s'mores on the beach.

I go to sail with my brothers. I go to develop relationships with my sisters-in-law and my nieces and nephews. I go because, in this fast-paced world, it's good to have a place to go where you're surrounded by family and life is simpler.

I discover that I feel best when I connect deeply through conversation and shared experiences with people I love and who love me back. That's why I keep going.

I go back so I can move forward in my life, secure in the knowledge that I'm loved by the great big group of men and women, boys and girls, who make up my family.

When I leave Cape Cod, I feel loved, I feel grateful, and I feel blessed. My parents have given me the gift of a beautiful family. I go back so I can move forward. It's that simple.

Dear God, thank you for the special relationship you have given me with my siblings. Help me to stay connected to them. Thank you for our shared history. Please help us to continue to be there for each other. Amen.

I'm Giving Up on Complaining

"True happiness comes not when we
get rid of all of our problems, but
when we change our relationship
to them, when we see our problems
as a potential source of awakening,
opportunities to practice patience,
and to learn."

—Richard Carlson

I have four brothers. No sisters, only brothers.

Every year without fail, when I go east to Cape Cod where we grew up, I spend time with all of them at once. When large families like ours get together, I find they often tell crazy stories that are funny to some members and not so funny to others. They rib one another, laugh at one another, stuff comes up, and yes, stuff comes out.

Lots of stuff.

On a recent trip, one of my brothers casually remarked, "Don't you think it's interesting that we sit around and complain about how our parents didn't do this and didn't do that, yet here we all are—all five of us together, talking and laughing with one another, working stuff out and through?"

Bingo! Whatever faults our parents had— and Lord knows everyone thinks their parents have faults (my kids included)— somehow ours did something really right. They encouraged us to stay together and stick together, and here we are.

On that trip, the same brother asked us if we thought "kids just always like to complain about their parents instead of trying to focus on what they did right?"

I thought about it, and it resonated as

true to me. We all complain. A lot. It seems so much easier to complain.

I complain about such stupid stuff. My kids do, too. I've been thinking about how really unattractive it is—at least to me—how utterly negative it is, and how I can choose to change it.

Like right now.

I decided I want to see if it makes me feel different to stop complaining. I'm going to tell my kids that I'm instituting a "complaint-free zone" in the house. In my office, too. In fact I'm going to try it for a year. (When I told that to a friend, she said, "Oh, Maria, get real! A year? How about one day at a time?")

Okay. Maybe that's more doable. One day at a time: No complaints about anything today. Not about friends or jobs, or what we're eating or not eating for dinner, or traffic, or what a sibling did or didn't do.

Not even about politics. Remember: if you don't like your elected officials, you can always get into the arena yourself.

One day at a time, out with the complaints both large and small, because those complaints affect my space, my day, my relationship with others, and my life. No more complaints about my age, my body, my work, my friends, and none about how I grew up or about what my parents didn't do right. It's so boring. After all, my kids are healthy, and so am I. I'm so very blessed, and I want to stay in that place of being grateful for my blessings. That feels so much better than whining.

Getting rid of the complaining allows me to move forward with gratitude. Especially to my parents for the greatest gift they gave me: the gift of friendship with my siblings.

I can only hope that way off in the distant future, when I'm long gone, that my own four kids are sitting together around a table sharing their lives and sharing stories about their childhood. I know that what I did wrong will come up, and I can hear that already. But I hope they'll also pause and realize, "Wow, look at us here—all together these many years later, sitting together, spending time together, laughing together. Our parents must have done something right!"

Dear God, please help me to stop complaining, to stop focusing on what's wrong, to stop zeroing in on what I regard as people's faults. Help me to focus instead on what's beautiful in my life and the gifts that have been given to me. Give me the grace to forgive others quickly and completely and to move forward in my life. Amen.

Six Family Truths
I've Learned Along the Way

"Love begins at home, and it is not
how much we do, but how much love
we put in the action that we do."
—Saint Teresa of Calcutta

People often ask me some variation of this question: "What do you think your parents did that helps keep all of you close as a family?"

I've thought long and hard about this myself, because I've always wanted to be sure my four children will stay as close and involved with each other long into the future as my brothers and I are.

I think the answer lies in a few things my mother used to say that have always stuck with me:

1. **"Loyalty to family."** My mother stressed this nonstop and also exemplified it in her own life. She was devoted to her parents and her siblings. She worked with them, played with them, and made it her business to stay connected to their business.

2. **"Find something to collaborate on with your siblings that is about making the world better."** My mother made my brothers and me work on the Special Olympics, the worldwide organization she started right in our backyard. It wasn't an option whether to be involved. She also made our friends get involved. Now all of my brothers run nonprofits. They work every day to make the world a more caring, compassionate, and conscious place, and I help them in any and every way I can, because I believe in what they're doing, and because I'm also trying to stay connected to what they're connected to. As my mother told us to do.

3. **"Don't come between your brothers and their spouses."** Really smart advice. I have four sisters-in-law. I love them all, and I've tried to develop my own relationships with them. But I also stay out of their relationships with my brothers. (Or at least I try!)

4. **"Support your siblings' families and develop relationships with their children."** We can all support our siblings by emotionally supporting their families—especially their kids—with our time, our wisdom, our joy. They are the next generation and the people to whom you'll help pass your family's values.

5. **"Make time for your siblings."** Gather with them as much as you can. My mother used to say, "You can fight with your brothers, you can beat them in sports [fat chance!], but never give up on them or lose contact with them." She said, "They

are more than friends. They are family. So make it work!"

And there's one more thing. My mother never told me this one. It's something I figured out on my own along the way:

6. **Don't discount or disparage their experiences.** Your siblings each have their own personal experiences with your parents and with one another. Listen to them, try to understand what they've been through and what they feel, and then work toward healing in a gentle, calm, nurturing, loving way. I've discovered that yelling, judging, screaming, insisting that "No, things were never ever that way!" never, ever works—especially with brothers, when you're the only girl. And if along the way, one of your siblings does confide in you, **do not** repeat what one sibling said about

the other to any of the rest. Respect confidentiality. Trust me on this.

One time when my brothers and I were all in the same place together, one of them quietly said to me and me alone, "You know, I think men today are more trapped than many women." He obviously wanted only me to hear him say that. That convinced me it's a good thing to give your siblings a safe space, a reassuring space, to talk. Just listen, and then hold your sibling like you would like to have been held by your mother or your father, and hold their experiences in your mind and your heart.

Bottom line: Wherever your siblings are, reach out to them, listen to them, hold them. The years and experiences you've shared are precious.

Dear God, with life as crazy busy as it is, I need to find ways to show my family they are more important to me than my work and other things that involve my time. Help me to plan one-on-one time with my brothers. Help me to continue to forge more wonderful new memories of sweet moments together. Amen.

We All Have Mental Health Issues. Here's Why It's Okay.

"People are scared to talk about it, but they should be scared about not talking about it."

—Prince Harry

Not too long ago, I was having a conversation with a friend when he said, "You know, every single person—yourself included—has mental health issues."

At first, I was surprised by his statement—even insulted by it. But as I reflected some more, I realized he was right.

Every single one of us does have mental health issues. Every single one of us has a mind, and we all need to think about preserving its health.

That's why I think the conversations Prince Harry and Prince William have ignited are so groundbreaking and important.

Prince Harry bravely told the world for the first time that grief over the death of his mother, Princess Diana, when he was twelve had wreaked havoc on his life for many years. He said that finally, when he felt close to emotional collapse after more than a decade of pushing the feelings down, his brother, Prince William, encouraged him to get professional help, which he did. Harry needed someone to give him the space and place where he could express his deepest feelings, and not worry about his confidentiality being broken.

I'm grateful that Prince William then used his own public platform to talk about how shock, grief, and trauma can live on in one's mind and body long after the initial insult took place, possibly producing post-traumatic stress issues and other mental health challenges.

Both of these young men gave us insight into how the shocking and violent death of their mother deeply affected their lives—admitting they had never even really talked about it to each other all those years.

As someone who also grew up in a public family that endured many traumatic events—where we also didn't talk about our feelings to anyone, either in the family or outside it—their revelations were liberating for me. To hear men talking bravely and openly about seeking professional help lifts the shame and stigma around mental health issues. When public people use their platform to spark awareness about an issue that needs to be out in the open, it's a gift to us all.

I have in my own way tried to do this. The very first book I wrote was a children's book about grief and death and the questions we all have about these once-taboo subjects. When I was First Lady of California, I moderated a moving conversation about grief at my Women's Conference. My mother had died two months before, and I was smack in the middle of it and needed to talk about it. As a mother, I talk openly with my kids about feelings and emotions, because I learned the consequences of growing up **not** doing that.

The fact is, life-altering events affect not just our hearts, but our mental well-being as well. The same event can affect different members of the same family in different ways. It's naive of us to think we can all just power on and power through trauma, in the mistaken belief that there are no lasting consequences.

My friend was right. We all have mental health issues. That doesn't make us weird or weak. It makes us human.

So next time someone tells you they have sought counseling—be it for the death of a loved one, the end of a marriage, the loss of a job, anxiety, depression, or whatever else they're dealing with—be compassionate. Be understanding.

After all, what Prince Harry said was both profound and telling: he just needed someone to listen.

Dear God, we all face life-altering events because we live in a world where terrible things happen and great loss results. Shock, grief, and trauma can produce times of darkness and deep discouragement long after the initial event. Because we are human, we are vulnerable. I am vulnerable. Thank you for leading me toward peace and hope in the midst of my brokenness. Help me not to withdraw into myself but rather to reach out to the right people when I need to. And help me to be gracious and compassionate to others in need, to listen, to support, and to protect. Amen.

Why We Should Stop Trying to "Go It Alone"

"No one heals himself by wounding another."

—Saint Ambrose

Every time I watch the news about the latest terrorist attack somewhere in the world, I experience a range of emotions. I feel shock. I feel angry. I feel fearful. I feel disbelief that this is happening yet again to innocent people, to our friends and allies. I feel horror that this is now our world, the one we all live in every day.

But then I take a deep breath and remind myself that there are far more good people in the world than bad, and that these incidents can bring out the best in all of us. So let's not give in to the fear that these terrorists are hoping we give in to. Let's not run, hide, or separate ourselves from our friends. Let us band together.

Watching these attacks unfold makes me think a lot about our country, our politics, but also about my own life.

Those who know me best would say I've always been a fiercely independent person. An only girl in a family of boys, I was always determined to chart my own course, to pave my own way and "go it alone."

Not too long ago, I said to one of my brothers, "I feel alone. I just wish I had help." He stopped me dead in my tracks by saying, "Maria, you have so much help all around you. You've always had help and support. You need to do a better job seeing the help that's already there for you and asking for the help you need."

He was right on both counts. Like many people, asking for help puts me outside my comfort zone. It makes me feel vulnerable. I like to do the helping, not the asking. I prefer the illusion of invulnerability.

But I've taken my brother's advice to heart. I've found myself asking for a lot of help lately with my work on Alzheimer's. I've asked family members to stand in for me in the cities where I couldn't show up at events. I've asked companies for their money and support. I've asked researchers to share their wisdom. I've asked, and I've asked, and I've asked.

It's never easy to ask for help, whether you're asking for a cause like Alzheimer's or for yourself when you just need someone to listen to you, to be there, and to lend support. If you're like me, asking feels like you're giving up that illusion of invulnerability. But that's what it is: an illusion. The fact is that asking for help requires strength. You have to be strong to step outside your comfort zone. It's humbling.

I've learned that not only can I ask for

help, I can also receive it. (I've got work to do on the receiving part, but I'm on it.) I've also learned that I can ask, be turned down, and survive. I've learned that I can rely on my family. I already knew this deep down, but asking them for help is new for me. I've learned that my friends are the "just say the word" type of friends. Without them, I'd be alone, and I've discovered that's a tough place to be.

I'm learning that there are so many people around me who are more than willing to help me. I just have to communicate what I need and slow down long enough to express my gratitude for their help. Expressing gratitude, my friends, is key.

I share my experience because perhaps, like me, asking for help and receiving it isn't your forte. If you are one of those "go it alone" types who's afraid to ask for help, take it from me: Going it alone is isolating, overwhelming, and most of all, it's unsustainable. And very often, it isn't the truth! So often when I prided myself on thinking I was going it alone, I wasn't. I've learned I've never accomplished anything of value without help.

Try to calm the anxious child in you that's telling you no one is there for you, no one can help you, and that you are all alone. Try to open your heart a bit wider, and you'll feel things you didn't feel before. Yes, some feelings may be painful, but better to know you can feel than to walk through life numb.

Which brings me back to our larger US. We, the United States of America, with all of our freedom and independence, have always been stronger and better when we are a part of a global community, one where we talk to others, listen to others, include others, and ask others for help. Being part of something larger than ourselves opens up our hearts and our minds.

As Pope Francis always reminds us, we

all share a common home: our planet. It's up to all of us to care for it. We all share a common longing to belong, to be seen, and to be accepted. We all share a common desire for friendship, for support, and for help. Going it alone—whether you are a person or a country—is an illusion. No one does anything alone. This I have learned. This I know deep in my heart.

So be strong enough to ask for help. Be vulnerable enough to share your needs and desires. And when someone helps you fulfill them, be brave enough to say thank you.

Because going it alone is so . . . silly. So yesteryear, so old-fashioned. Be modern! Ask for help. That goes not just for people, but for communities. I know I need it. So do our friends around the world—especially those who are under attack.

Be open to help, be willing to ask for it, be brave enough to be grateful for it, and be generous enough to give it.

Dear God, our culture exalts the outwardly strong, independent people who chart their own course, pave their own way, and "go it alone." But the truth is that no one really does anything alone, and to try is overwhelming, isolating, and exhausting. I struggle with weakness, shortcomings, and inadequacies, and yet I resist asking for help. Please teach me to humble myself and cultivate the practice of seeking help from others and from you. I open my heart to receiving and giving help, and I ask your forgiveness for those times I have tried to handle it all on my own. Amen.

Looking for the Light
in the Cracks

"The most important thing in life is
to learn how to give out love, and to
let it come in."

—Morrie Schwartz

As the noise of the news continues to get louder, meaner, more confusing, more divisive, more violent, and more heartbreaking, I have found myself trying to look for the cracks in between.

Yes, the cracks. As singer-songwriter Leonard Cohen wrote in his song "Anthem," "There is a crack in everything. That's how the light gets in."

Lately, I've been choosing to widen my gaze beyond the daily news I consume and seek out the good—the light, the love, and the truth—that's shining through the cracks. Surprisingly, I don't have to look very far, because I see so many great examples of light, love, and integrity everywhere I look. Yes, I do.

I hear songs about love. I read about concerts celebrating oneness and marches for tolerance and understanding. I meet people who are doing their best to help their communities and be of service to humanity.

Right now, I find myself trying to turn away from the grown men and women who routinely hurl insults at one another on social media and TV. I find myself turning away from those in Washington, DC, who seem to delight in the "he said/she said" wars, while millions of our fellow citizens are struggling. They're struggling in unsafe neighborhoods and schools. They're struggling to survive paycheck to paycheck. And they're living in fear that they will lose their health care or other vital services.

Sure, I still follow the news. I'm a journalist and a citizen, and I want to be informed. I just don't want to be taken down by what I'm witnessing play out in our politics and our national dialogue. Instead, I'm choosing to focus on the examples of love that I see, because that's what reinforces my belief in humanity. That's what inspires me to work harder, do more, and focus on hope even more.

Now, I know the word **love** gets thrown around a lot, and I myself have struggled with it in my life. But it's still my favorite four-letter word! Thank God I know what it feels like to be loved. Thank God for the opportunity we all have to spread love whenever we can, because I know it's the healing and unifying connection we're all seeking. And yet, it seems to slip away so easily. Why is that?

Why is exhibiting love sometimes harder to do than exhibiting meanness? Why do bullying, grandstanding, and powermon-gering so often take precedence over love? Why do so few leaders talk of love? Why do so few leaders exhibit it on the world stage for us to witness? Is it because being loving is regarded as weak or soft?

It's not. As my friend Elizabeth Lesser once said, love is a muscular concept. It takes strength to give love and to receive it. It takes strength to pursue it and to make it a guiding value in your life.

I don't know about you, but I'm so over the meanness, the negativity, and the gas-lighting. I'm so over leaders who threaten or intimidate. I don't want leaders without any emotional intelligence. I don't want leaders who are too scared to even talk of love, much less lead with love. I just don't, and I'm not afraid to say it.

The good news is that looking between the cracks gives us glimpses of the leaders among us who are leading with love and who have the guts to say so. They are there, and they, not the screamers, are the ones with strength.

So, my fellow citizens, if you have love in your heart, step up and step out. You are what the world needs now more than ever. Love is the most powerful weapon on the planet. Imagine if we all decided to lead with it.

As Martin Luther King Jr. once said: "We shall match your capacity to inflict suffering by our capacity to endure suffering. . . . Do to us what you will and we will still love you."

Imagine if we all spoke from that space. Imagine if we all interacted from that space. Imagine if we all approached one another with love, light, and truth.

It is within us. We just need to let it rise to the top and lead with it. We need our leaders to lead with it.

Love: it's our best defense, and it's the

only way all this other noise will fade into the background.

Dear God, thank you that you are the God of love and that your love is the light that shines in this present darkness. May it shine into my heart and give me the strength and compassion to love others like you do. There is no weapon and no instrument for change on our planet more powerful than your love. Amen.

One Person Can Make a Huge Impact on You

"I have one life and one chance to make it count for something. . . . My faith demands that I do whatever I can, wherever I am, whenever I can, for as long as I can with whatever I have to try to make a difference."
—**President Jimmy Carter**

One person can change your life. Pope Francis has changed mine.

I got into journalism long ago because I wanted to cover stories that could inspire people. I've covered a lot of big events in my career and interviewed a lot of people, but covering Pope Francis's visit to America was without a doubt one of the all-time highlights.

I didn't interview him, and I never shook his hand. But that doesn't matter, because as I followed him and covered all the stops on his trip, his words touched my heart and ignited my spirit. I felt them deep in my soul. Every sermon, every speech he gave moved me more.

When he spoke at the 9/11 Memorial, the NBC News studio fell silent, all of us transfixed as he spoke about pain, remembrance, and the power of love. I listened as he read the Prayer of Saint Francis and the Beatitudes, and it brought me to tears. I watched as leaders of so many different faiths stood up beside him and spoke their truth. I thought about how I'm living my own life.

Later on the trip, when the Pope spoke to Congress about the Golden Rule, I thought about his message and how well I'm living it. When he urged us to all go out and be of service, I took a personal inventory of myself, and I knew that I could do better.

In fact, the whole week made me take an internal inventory of everything in my life. It made me reassess power, success, money, joy, work, and love.

I'm still thinking about the power of his call for Americans to adopt "a culture of care—care for oneself, care for others, care for the environment—in the place of a culture of waste, a throwaway culture." Wow.

Pope Francis pushes us to realize that we're all sharing a common home, a home we must care for, respect, love, and honor. He pushes us to open our eyes and our hearts to our neighbors, especially those living on the margins—who live so close, yet whom we may keep outside our consciousness. He challenges us to help real men and real women get out of extreme poverty. He says, "To enable them to escape poverty, we must allow them to be dignified agents of their destiny." I love that. He's saying every single one of us should have the wherewithal to be dignified agents of our own destiny.

I love this man. I love the way he speaks, the wisdom he shares, the gentle but strong and clear way he asks each of us for more.

I believe deeply that the world is yearning to be good, to be better and do better than we currently are. I believe in the goodness of people. I believe in their kindness. I saw it everywhere I went while following the Pope around the United States. I believe all of us who hear him—no matter what our religious belief—feel like he is speaking directly to us, and that makes us feel validated, felt, and seen. We all share a common desire to be understood, to be loved, to be accepted, and to be treated like we matter.

You don't have to meet a great leader in person or talk to him one-on-one to be transformed. A great leader reaches out, listens, feels your pain, and works to make it bearable. A great leader ignites your heart. He inspires you to want to be a better person. A great leader can heal.

"Pray for me," Pope Francis says to those he meets along his way, and then he says, "To those who don't believe, I hope you wish me well." I hope that we all dig down and find the strength to wish one another well. It's so simple. It's so profound. It's so Pope Francis!

In Philadelphia, the Pope told the story of the Pennsylvanian Saint Katharine Drexel, who had a private audience with Pope Leo XIII in 1887. She told him of the challenges faced by Native Americans and African Americans back home. She asked him to send Catholic missionaries to come help these people. The Pope asked her: "**What about you?** What are **you** going to do?"

The question made her think about her own contribution to the Church, and she made a decision to change her life. She took her vows, founded the Sisters of the Blessed Sacrament, and devoted her life to speaking out against racial injustice and helping and educating American Indians and African Americans. Saint Katharine Drexel was canonized by Pope John Paul II in 2000.

"What about you? What are you **going to do?"** The question goes deep. What can you and I do to make our communities better, more compassionate, kinder, and more caring? What can we each do to care for our common home?

As Pope Francis said, it's up to each and every one of us to lead. It's up to each and every one of us to decide to walk through the world with humility, tenderness, and a respect for the Other. It's doubly important to do this, he said, if you're in any position of power.

I thank Pope Francis for leading with humility, with simplicity, and with empathy and love. And as he asked of us, I pray for him. I'm praying for Pope Francis and praying for you. Please pray for me, too. Amen.

Dear God, help me to confidently answer the calling to help make the world a better place by being caring, tender, and respectful toward others. Help me to be the best version of the person you created me to be. Amen.

Men and Kindness

"Love and kindness are never wasted. They always make a difference. They bless the one who receives them, and they bless you, the giver."
—Barbara De Angelis

Love and kindness are the guiding principles of the type of society I want to live in. I believe kindness is one of the most important qualities we can have. It's what can lead us out of the screaming and yelling and negativity that characterize our current atmosphere, which is anything but kind.

But lovingkindness is not just a guiding principle, an ideal, and a goal. I believe it should be the leading edge of the way we actually connect with one another.

And I'm not just talking about women! We shouldn't regard kindness as a positive attribute only of women. It's an attribute of admirable men, too—**strong** admirable men. Because it takes great strength—maybe **especially** if you're a man—to think enough of yourself to put yourself out there in the world as kind and caring. So many men think that if they're kind, they just may get walked on or over. But it takes true strength to be sure of yourself and not so terribly worried and fearful that people will think you're weak or wishy-washy if you're kind.

All—and I mean all—the truly strong men I have known in my life have been kind. They don't mistake cruelty or inattention or steeliness as necessary hallmarks of masculinity. They think enough of themselves as men to be kind to others. Kind fathers raise strong daughters, and kind fathers raise strong men who feel good about themselves.

The fact is, things are changing. Being a

good father has become an accepted attribute of good men. Today when I go out for a walk, I see men pushing baby carriages. I see them carrying diaper bags, showing up in record numbers at school functions, and showing up in equal numbers at their daughters' and sons' games.

I hear men talk about their emotional intelligence. I hear men talking about their children and how they want to be more attuned, more involved, and, yes, kinder.

So I want to shine a light on men who are talking openly and honestly about their experiences as fathers, about what they learned from their own fathers, and about how they're using what they've learned to help others. I want to shine a light on fathers who are leading from a strong place: a place of kindness.

Build me a son, O Lord, whose heart will be clear, whose goal will be high;

a son who will master himself before he seeks to master other men; one who will reach into the future, yet never forget the past. . . . Give him humility, so that he may always remember the simplicity of true greatness, the open mind of true wisdom, and the weakness of true strength.

—General Douglas MacArthur

A Message from My Mother
I Will Cherish Forever

"Love is the strongest force the world possesses and yet it is the humblest imaginable."

—Mahatma Gandhi

I've been desperately trying to tidy up, to clear out so much of the stuff I've collected through the years. The goal: keeping only those things that spark joy.

So I start with my books. I love books. So I look at them one at a time and separate them into piles: keep this, donate that.

Suddenly it happens: I came upon a book I discovered had been inscribed to me by my mother. Now, over my lifetime, I got many, many books from my mother. But this inscription—which I had never seen or read—stops me cold, and I burst into tears. Why? Because the truth of it hits me right in the gut:

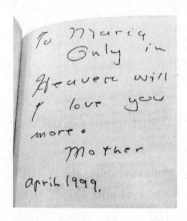

To Maria.
Only in
Heaven will
I love you
more.
        Mother.

Now, I have no doubt that my mother loved me here on earth. But she was so tough, so relentless, so driven, that she showed her love by pushing you and driving you forward. There's no doubt in my mind that she wanted to love all of us in a gentler way, but she didn't know how. She wasn't raised like that.

So seeing her message to me these many

years later in her own handwriting tells me her truth: that she can love me more from Heaven, where she is free to love in a different way.

Not a day goes by when I don't miss my mother, when I don't want to talk to her about something. Finding this book with her message in it makes me feel connected to her in such a beautifully profound way. It takes the edge off the grief.

I've written about grief quite a bit, as I struggle to make sense of it. In fact, as I've said, the first book I ever wrote was a children's book about grief, death, loss, Heaven, and the questions a child has about it all. They are the same questions we have as adults, yet we don't often create an open space to talk about such pain in adulthood. Grieving is such a personal experience. It's a journey into unknowing, into faith, into letting go, and into acceptance. It's hard.

But now here I am—a space opened up

wide for me to talk about it, a space created by opening up a book I had stashed away. A book with a message I didn't know about and needed to hear, a message of love from my mother to me that's been in my home all along. Now that message is in my heart forever.

So I'm grateful I started tidying up. I'm grateful I'm looking at each book before deciding whether to throw it out. If not, I would have missed one of the most profound messages I've ever been given in my life: that I am loved, both on this earth and from Heaven.

Dear God, thank you for unexpected gifts of love that are all around me. May I continue to stay open to finding them, seeing them, and letting them into my heart. Amen.

Finding Peace in Your Decisions

> "Life is full of tough decisions,
> and nothing makes them easy. . . .
> Try, trust, try, and trust again, and
> eventually you'll feel your mind
> change its focus to a new level of
> understanding."
>
> **—Martha Beck**

I was educated and deeply shaped by the Catholic sisters and the Jesuits. Pope Francis is one of the individuals I admire most in the world, not just because he is a Jesuit, but because of the way he walks his talk, lives his life, speaks his mind, and embraces change.

When faced with difficult decisions or life-altering change, the Jesuits have a process to help guide them to the answer. Devised by Saint Ignatius Loyola, the founder of the Jesuits, it's called the **Process of Discernment**. It walks you through a step-by-step procedure that helps you come to the decision that's right for you.

The truth is, some of us are better than others at making good decisions. Some of us make snap decisions. Some labor forever, weighing the pros and cons into the ground. Some take too many other people's opinions and feelings into account (that would be me). But there are some who just know how to discern, deliberate, and decide.

I talk about the Process of Discernment today because making big decisions is tough for everyone, and so many people I've spoken to tell me they're struggling with it right now. So, I thought, why not take a page from the Jesuits and follow their age-old, tried-and-true formula? I've used it myself for decision making in the past, and recently, I've been using it again to make some new decisions.

So the next time you're unclear about a decision, Google the Jesuits' Process of Discernment and try it out. It may help you find clarity and peace. I've found the process illuminating and helpful when some turbulence in my life provokes a crisis of indecision. The process includes steps like these:

- Identify the decision to be made or the issue to be resolved.

- Formulate the issue in a proposal.

- Pray for openness and freedom.

- Gather all the necessary information.

- Discuss the matter with someone sensitive to your values.

- Repeat step three above.

- And one I find very helpful: Observe the direction of your own will (your own desires) while reflecting on the advantages and disadvantages of it.

- Trust in God and make your decision, even if you're not certain about it.

- Live with the decision for a while to see if your thoughts, desires, and feelings continue to support it. If not, redo the process.

Discern. Decide. Be at peace with your decision, and allow others to do and be the same.

Dear God, I struggle with making decisions. I worry that I will make the wrong ones, so I get paralyzed and make no decisions at all. Please help me change this. Please help me take the action of making my decision and leaving the results to you. I know that no matter what happens, you will help me. Amen.

Why We Need Time to Think and Reflect

"You have to go internal if you want to go eternal."

—Sargent Shriver

I learned something recently in two separate conversations I'll never forget. Both California Governor Jerry Brown and former Secretary of State George Shultz spoke to me about how important it's been throughout their lives and careers to set aside uninterrupted time in their busy days—time to be, to think, to reflect. Each went on to explain how difficult it is to safeguard that alone time, but also how critical it has been to his thinking and his ability to create and lead.

I loved that simple but profound advice.

No matter how busy you are, carve out time in your day to get calm, to be present, to think, to reflect.

I'm grateful I heard that advice from them right before I went onstage to speak, because it helped me to stay present. It helped me to stay in the moment. It allowed me to take in what was actually happening right then, when it was happening.

So when I sat there onstage looking out at the audience, I was overcome with gratitude—gratitude to my parents, gratitude to my family, and gratitude to all who have impacted my life. So many people have helped me and continue to help me in so many ways. Being present also allowed me to take in the love that's been there for me in my life—and was there for me that night. I didn't push it away, as I might have in the past. I let it in, and it felt beautiful. And because I was present for it, that was a moment I will never forget.

When I went back to my hotel, I made a vow to myself. I promised to create more empty space in my days. More time to think. To dream. To be calm. To just be, so that I can be more present in my own life.

I think we are at a unique moment in our fast-paced, ever-changing world. I think our world needs us all to be more present, to be calmer, more reflective, more creative. If we each made an effort to carve out that space in our daily lives, I have no doubt that our interactions with one another would be different. I have no doubt we would see differently, hear differently, and realize different things. I have no doubt that we would show up in our lives in a different way, speak up in a different way, and perhaps help move our country forward together in the way we all say we want it to go.

That's something worth thinking about, reflecting on, and being present for.

Dear God, help me to take time every day to be alone with you and shut out everything else but your presence. Help me to experience your presence in my life and to hear your voice speaking in my heart. Amen.

Mother's Day Every Day

"The best way to find yourself is to
lose yourself in the service of others."
—attributed to Mahatma Gandhi

What I've learned in my decades of mothering is that mothering requires work, thought, and energy, 24/7. It requires you to show up as both gentle and tough, kind and strong, patient and unconditionally loving. It requires you to do all of this without allowing anyone to walk all over you. And if you have more than one child, it requires that you adjust and be creative, because just as no two children are exactly the same (even twins, I hear!), no two children can be mothered in exactly the same way. What works for one doesn't necessarily work for the other.

But today, I want to move beyond my own intimate experience with motherhood and focus on what I believe the world at large is yearning for right now. Simply put, that's Mothering with a capital M, Mothering on a big stage and on a big scale.

What do I mean by that? I mean that I believe all of the world's children—young and old—are looking to be loved, accepted, nurtured, soothed, and cared for by Mother energy.

Really good mothers make really good leaders because they nurture, they build a solid team, they see your potential, and they build on your strengths, not on your fears. They inspire you, they guide you, and they ask of you. Plus, they're really strong, so you shouldn't mess with them.

I loved it when the president of France said in his acceptance speech that he would govern with humility, devotion, and determination, and also that he would "serve with love."

That's what mothers do every day. Day in and day out, mothers serve with humility, devotion, determination, and love.

May we all realize that mothering is a presidential-level task that, done right, can lead a family, a nation, or a world to fulfill its highest potential.

So it's not just on Mother's Day that we should honor mothering for what it is: the hardest job in the world. It's one that deserves our respect, our devotion, and our love every day.

Mothering: It's a muscular job. It takes balls.

Dear God, you said that your Son came to earth to be a servant to all the world's children—the young and the old alike. He loved, accepted, nurtured, soothed,

and cared for them in the grandest way. I
want to serve with love as well. Help me
to be both gentle and strong and to speak
words that lift up and not tear down, that
build confidence and strength. May I be
patient and love others unconditionally.
Please take my simple acts of service and
transform them into something influential
and purposeful that can help and
encourage others. Amen.

We're All in This Together

"All of our humanity is dependent upon recognizing the humanity in others."
—Archbishop Desmond Tutu

The news of the day is rarely simple and/or great, no matter how much we wish it to be. I find that people want it to be black versus white, right versus wrong. But it rarely is. Your take on the news depends so much on what you've experienced in life. You and I can look at the same picture, read the same story, or listen to the same speech, and yet have completely different takes on what is being said and what it means.

I am connected to you, and yes, you are

connected to me. We share the same planet. We breathe the same air. How I treat me is how I should strive to treat you. What I want for my family is what I should strive to want for your family—regardless of your religion, the color of your skin, your gender, your sexual orientation, or your political affiliation. I long to drop the labels we use to identify ourselves and that we so often hide behind, as they always seem to take us further from one another, instead of closer together.

So as we heatedly debate the news of the day—as we're flooded with images of people crying for help—may we stop and remember that we're all together in this great big family called the human race.

Our future depends on seeing our common humanity and finding ways to elevate it and move it forward toward a better place than where it is today. We're not here to destroy one another. We're here to connect with one another and to help one another. Our very survival depends on one another.

This week, I've been thinking about the power of prayer. I'm a big believer in the power of prayer, because I've seen it work firsthand. In fact, right now I'm a part of a prayer circle for a friend battling cancer, and I know it's effective, because she's still out there running around, working, and being a warrior for social justice.

I pray every morning and every evening to settle myself, to guide myself, to focus myself, to express gratitude, and to be in conversation with God. I pray for myself, for my children, for my friends, and yes, for those I seek to better understand—including those I don't understand, because they see things differently from the way I see them.

I'm going to keep praying for all of us and for our shared humanity. It's there for us to see. All we need to do is open our eyes, our minds, and our hearts and let it in.

Dear God, when my problems seem overwhelming, I trust you to take care of what I cannot. I choose to fix my gaze on you and trust in your mighty power. I know that nothing will happen that is outside of your knowledge or control. Teach me to find shelter in your presence, to follow you one day at a time, and to take the steps that will overcome the challenges I face. Amen.

"We Are the Ones
We've Been Waiting For"

"One person can make a difference,
and everyone should try."
—**President John F. Kennedy**

I've tried to spend less time worrying and
more time reflecting. Not just reflecting
back on what was, but reflecting on how
I want to move my life forward.

I know I want to move forward with
hope. I want to move forward with faith. I
want to move forward with conviction, passion, and purpose. I know I want to use my
voice clearly and confidently on behalf of
the people and issues I care about.

I want to use my voice to move the needle
when it comes to understanding the beautiful human mind and why we're losing so

very many of them to Alzheimer's. This disease is wiping out so many of our mothers, our daughters, our sisters, our brothers, our fathers, and our families. It's wiping them out financially, emotionally, physically, and spiritually. I firmly believe that we, in turn, can wipe out this mind-blowing disease, and I will not rest until we do so. I believe that is my part in making this a more caring, conscious, and compassionate world. I don't find myself discouraged by the enormity of the challenge. I find myself invigorated by it, because I believe the goal is attainable.

On the wall in my office hangs a poem that deeply inspires me every time I read it. It's a poem that moves me to get moving. It gives me a sense of urgency, and it speaks to my heart and to my mind.

It is attributed to an elder of the Hopi tribe in Arizona, and it speaks to the leader who lives in each of us. It speaks to the power of the individual, the need for community, and the urgency of Now. It challenges us not to sit by and wait for someone else to lead us forward:

A Hopi Elder Speaks

"You have been telling the people that this is the Eleventh Hour.

Now you must go back and tell the people that this is the Hour.

And there are things to be considered . . .

Where are you living?

What are you doing?

What are your relationships?

Are you in right relation?

Where is your water?

Know your garden.

It is time to speak your Truth.

Create your community.

Be good to each other.

And do not look outside yourself for the leader."

Then he clasped his hands together, smiled, and said, "This could be a good time!

"There is a river flowing now very fast. It is so great and swift that there are those who will be afraid. They will try to hold on to the shore. They will feel they are torn apart and will suffer greatly.

"Know the river has its destination. The elders say we must let go of the shore, push off into the middle of the river, keep our eyes open, and our heads above water. And I say, see who is in there with you and celebrate. At this time in history, we are to take nothing personally, least of all ourselves. For the moment that we do, our spiritual growth and journey comes to a halt.

"The time for the lone wolf is over. Gather yourselves! Banish the word **struggle** from your attitude and your vocabulary. All that we do now must be done in a sacred manner and in celebration.

"We are the ones we've been waiting for."

**—attributed to the Hopi Nation
Oraibi, Arizona**

So if you find yourself at this moment in your life reflecting on what was and what is, take a page from the Hopi Elder. Speak your truth. At this time in our lives, we are to take nothing personally, least of all ourselves. The time of the lone wolf is over. This is the hour. We are indeed the ones we have been waiting for.

Something to Focus on Other Than Your Lips, Thighs, and Eyes

"Although no one can go back and make a brand new start, anyone can start from now and make a brand new ending."

—Carl Bard

I don't care what you wear or don't wear. I don't care how much you spend on makeup or eyelashes. I don't care if you've had plastic surgery or want to in the future. I don't care if you've been divorced, dropped out of work to raise your kids, or worked like a lunatic your entire life.

I don't care if you're a Democrat, a Republican, an Independent, a Green, or a Decline-to-State. I don't care what your job is, how much money you make, or who you know or don't know. I don't care if you're Catholic, Buddhist, Jewish, Protestant, or atheist. I don't care if you identify as male or female, gay or straight or "other," black, white, brown, or none of the above.

I really don't care.

What I do care about is your mind, and I want to get into it. I care not just during Mental Health Awareness Month, although I do care deeply about mental health. I care because I want to help you protect your mind and make it last a lifetime.

Every sixty-six seconds, a new brain develops Alzheimer's disease. Two-thirds of those brains belong to women, and no one knows why that is. To me, and I hope to you as well, that's unacceptable.

I've made it my mission to find out why Alzheimer's is robbing so many people—so many women!—of their minds in the prime of their lives. I've seen the scourge of this disease up close in my own family, and I don't want **you** to have to experience losing your mind or to have to watch someone you love lose theirs. Take my word for it, it's a truly mind-blowing process to witness.

Alzheimer's is the most expensive health crisis facing our nation, and we have to stop it. We can stop it by continuing to fund the research so critical to advancing our understanding of this devastating disease.

My mother always drilled into me the importance of developing my mind. She'd say, "Maria, your looks will go, but if you develop your brain, it will last as long as you do and make all the difference in your life."

So, while I **am** trying to hold on to my looks as long as I can (haha), I'm primarily focused on my brainpower—and yours. I care deeply about both.

Our minds are something we all have in common. Together, we can save them.

Dear God, please guide me toward better health, to eat well, to exercise well, to learn more, and to be social as well. Hold my life in your hands and renew my mind, body, soul, and spirit. With you, all things are possible. Amen.

Reflections on a Whirlwind Week

"There is no greater reward than
working from your heart, and
making a difference in the world."
                    —Carlos Santana

Have you ever had one of those weeks when no matter how hard you try to stay upbeat, cheery, and positive, you just can't? Of course you have. That's what this past week has felt like for me.

This was one of those weeks when events unfolded so rapidly, it was hard to keep up. I spoke to folks who were glued to the news and social media, trying to dissect it all in real time and figure out what it all meant. Meanwhile, others I spoke to said they just couldn't bear any of it and turned off everything electronic.

These are confusing and chaotic times, for sure. Few things feel certain anymore. It's hard to see a clear path ahead. It's hard to know what to think when everything seems to be changing more rapidly than the time it takes to form a new thought. That's why during times like these, I try to spend some time away from the noise so that I can better clarify what I really **do** think.

And how do I do that? I read and listen to others whose words and thoughts lift me up and help focus my mind on the positive. That doesn't mean I'm naive. It's simply means I'm acknowledging that we can choose how we respond to all the noise and change swirling around.

I reach out to those whom I respect, people I feel can offer perspective. They remind me that we've gone through tumultuous times like these before. The turbulent 1960s. Assassinations. Vietnam. Watergate. A president's resignation. Iran-Contra. Horrendous natural disasters. September 11th. And on and on. Clarity and calm always comes back to us, but it takes time.

So give yourself permission to step away. Breathe. Turn to those with wisdom who have seen it all and lived to tell it. Stay attuned to the news, yes, but don't allow yourself to become sucked into and consumed by it either.

Find your resolve. Focus on the good you can do in your own life. Our communities, our country need the good we have to offer. They need for us to turn down the volume on the nastiness and look forward to a future that's more united than divided. I think we can all agree that we deserve a future that's more bright than dark, more positive than negative, more compassionate than critical.

I'm focused on moving us forward and uniting us. Will you join me?

Dear God, help me to step away from the noise today, take a deep breath, quiet my heart and mind, and trust you to take care of all the uncertainty I feel about what I cannot control. Keep me from fear and discouragement when the path ahead is hidden and confusing. Thank you for all the wise people you have given to me whose words and actions lift me above the negative and the critical and bring the clarity and positive perspective I need. Help me to stop and listen to them and to remember what they've said, so that I can refocus on the good that I can do for others. Even though I don't see the path ahead, I rest assured that my future is in your hands. Amen.

My Easter Reflections

"He is not here. He has risen!"
—**Luke 24:6**

E aster is all about rising. I'm not just talking about Jesus rising from the dead, although that's my metaphor. I'm talking about the fact that today can be a moment when each of us chooses to rise in our own lives.

My brother Timothy asked me for time we could spend together. So off we went to spend a weekend at a retreat in New Mexico organized by Father Richard Rohr. We went to listen, to learn, to connect, to be with one another, and to be at one with ourselves. (His beautiful daughter Rose came with us, too.)

Father Rohr was joined by William Paul Young, author of **The Shack**, and Cynthia

Bourgeault, an Episcopal priest and modern-day mystic.

The weekend was moving, meaningful, and profound, culminating in a beautiful mass. It gave me time to think about my own story and to think about the highs and lows of life—not just my own, but all of ours. For as Father Rohr said, if you have a soul, then you must acknowledge that everyone else does, too. They also have highs and lows and dark and light.

My time with these wonderful souls was life-affirming.

Here are twenty of the takeaways I brought home with me:

1. What is broken in you makes you human, not bad. We're all united in our brokenness and in our suffering. Acknowledge it.
2. Revelations happen from the inside out, not the outside in. Allow for them.

3. We think we need to know someone before we can love them, but divine thinking is to love **before** you know. Love unconditionally.

4. One of the biggest challenges we face today is loss of meaning. Find meaning wherever you can.

5. Religion has become too centered on sins. We were taught that our sins separate us from God, but that's not true.

6. If you always have to convince your parents to love you, then you never trust that they do. Note to parents: Focus on giving the love your child is seeking.

7. There are moments in all of our lives when we are blind, and then we see. Open your mind to other ways of thinking and seeing. That will get you out of the dualistic frame of mind that sees everything as good versus bad or right versus wrong. Open your mind to a third way.

8. The contemplative mind approaches things in their completeness. Be contemplative in action. Contemplation and action actually do go together.

9. Most thinking is simply the result of an obsessive mind. Find ways to turn yours off.

10. You have to pull the rug out from under yourself. Only then can you live in the flow. In choosing to accept the unknowing that life presents, you'll be able to accept the flow.

11. Wholeness is when the way of your being matches the truth of your being. And the truth is, you are a very good creation. Note to self: Accept this truth as it is.

12. The opposite of "more" is "enough." Remember that.

13. In order for your "yes" to matter, your "no" has to matter, too.

14. Everything comes down to your capacity

for presence. Your mind dwells in the past and the future. Work with it to focus on the present.

15. Most of us carry shame in our bodies, so we punish them for it. Integrating your mind and body helps you to be present.

16. See yourself as doing God's work. When you see yourself this way, see others as doing God's work, too.

17. We often hold on to other people's stories of ourselves. Know your own story and tell it.

18. Electricity can operate only in a circuit. There has to be a giver and a receiver. Remember that.

19. You will know what you need to know when you need to know it.

20. Your experiences are yours and yours alone. Each and every one of us has a mission, a purpose, and a calling. Our challenge on this day and all days is to rise to that calling.

The final thought I will leave you with today is this: I would never have gone to this retreat had my brother Timothy not asked me to set aside some time to spend with him. I'm so glad he did. So when someone you love asks you for time, take it. You will have your own glorious list of takeaways.

Dear God, I celebrate you as the God of resurrection. There are dreams I have had and areas of my life that seem to have withered away and died long ago, but you have the power to help me bring them back to life. You will always bring new paths to walk, and your grace is always fresh and overflowing. Amen.

A Time to Rest

"Each day, each of us is faced with the possibility of resetting our lives. Refocusing. Reimagining. Rebooting. Every day, we can decide to change our outlook, our words, our tone, and our attitude."

—Maria

Reflect. Remember. Rest. Recharge. That's what I want to do, because I feel that everything is moving way too fast—our politics, our conversations, our relationships, and our lives.

When everyone is in such a hurry, balls inevitably get dropped, hurtful things get said, misunderstandings occur, and crazy things happen. And no one takes the time to say, "Hey, wait a minute!"

What are we doing? What are we thinking? Where are we going? Let's stop. Let's rest a minute. Let's reflect on what's happening now and what's already happened. Let's take a beat and gather ourselves, so that we can refocus, recharge, and move forward in a more unified way.

I mean this sincerely and seriously. It's time for all of us—regardless of our age, sex, race, gender, or political leanings—to be more conscious, more considerate, and more compassionate, not to mention less angry and judgmental.

Now, before you scream, "How can she talk about resting when bombs are going off that are killing young children? When politicians are threatening to cut programs that for many mean the difference between life and death? When the ice caps are melting? When Washington is embroiled in fighting and one-upping and name-calling and stonewalling? When the world feels like it's coming apart at the seams?"

Well, I would suggest that this is exactly the moment when we do, in fact, need to rest.

Now, resting isn't something I grew up with. In fact, I think it's fair to say it was scorned in my home. If either of my parents saw anyone resting—well, let's just say that no one would have dared try.

But I've come to realize that resting is of value. Stopping to rest doesn't mean you're weak or too tired to go on. It doesn't mean something is wrong with you or that you're un-American (even if Americans like to think of themselves as the most competitive and hard-driven people on the planet).

Rest is important for your mind, your body, and your heart. When you rest, you can recharge and refocus. You can dream, tap into your consciousness and creative spirit. You can get in touch with yourself and your own purpose and mission.

The truth is, I've done a lot of running around in my life, only to learn that the most successful people get more done when they have taken time to slow down.

When people have stopped to rest, they are more thoughtful, they are more focused, and they are more at peace with themselves and those around them. They are also better parents, better partners, and better professionals. People who make time to rest get stuff done—and they do it without creating chaos and carnage in their wake.

So before you say to yourself, "I can't rest. I just don't have time to reflect or recharge. I have too much to do . . ." take it from me. I'm someone who would have said those same words a few years ago. But I've learned this: We're all going to end up in the same place anyway, so what's the rush?

On this Memorial Day weekend, the unofficial start of summer, I'm going to make rest part of my time off. In fact, I'm going to make it part of my summer and my life.

I'm also going to spend time this weekend

remembering all of the brave military men and women who have given their lives for our country. I want to pay my respects to them and express my gratitude to their families who get left behind and too often struggle alone to put the pieces back together.

A recent Memorial Day weekend marked what would have been the 100th birthday of my uncle President John F. Kennedy. I took the time to reflect on his legacy and what he fought for in World War II, what he stood for in his political life, and why his words still have such an impact today.

That made me think, "What is it that **I** stand for? What am **I** doing for my country? How am **I** giving back? How am **I** serving the common good?" (Complaining or railing on Twitter doesn't count as serving the common good, by the way.)

Please stop and reflect on who and what is important to you. Please reflect on why you do what you do.

Recharge your batteries. Refocus your resolve. Remember that you are among the blessed. You are still here, so you still have a shot at making an impact with your life and benefiting others. Why not take it? Take time to stop and rest now. Because, trust me, we still have a lot of work to do.

Dear God, it feels as though the world is coming apart at the seams, and my world of constant motion is spinning with stress. You taught us that you wanted us to slow down sometimes and get rest for body and soul and mind and spirit, to recharge our batteries and refocus our resolve. Help me to stop and reflect on what I am doing, and why I am doing it, and to know my purpose and mission in this life. Help me to be still and know that you are God and to hear you speak, so that I can move forward with strength and confidence. Amen.

What I'm Grateful for This Thanksgiving

"Sally, Thanksgiving is a very important holiday. Ours was the first country in the world to make a national holiday to give thanks."
—**Charles M. Schulz**

Thanksgiving is my favorite holiday, because it celebrates what's important in my life: family, friends, faith—and food! I should throw in football, because that's always part of Thanksgiving in our house, too.

Thanksgiving is about gratitude. It's about gathering. It's not about wrapping and unwrapping presents. It's about being present in our loved ones' lives.

Every year I used to go home to Washington to celebrate Thanksgiving with my parents. It was something I counted on and looked forward to every year: seeing my brothers and their families, my dad carving the turkey, and my mother's face wreathed in joy as she sat at the head of the table, both of them basking in the love and laughter of the family they built.

After they both passed away and my own family situation changed, I found myself struggling to come up with a new Thanksgiving tradition. At first I was invited to my friend's Thanksgiving celebrations. But then I realized it had always been such an important holiday to me that I wanted to start my own tradition. How to do that? Well, one thing I always admired about my parents' Thanksgiving is that they included anyone and everyone their children wanted to invite. So I started doing that, too. Slowly but surely, my table filled up, and slowly but surely a new tradition was born.

What happens at Thanksgiving is powerful. I've often had people at my table who weren't born here, who weren't raised knowing about this holiday, but who've come to love it, because it's about being welcomed at the table. It's about acceptance. It's about being invited in.

Gather at the table. Invite people in. Celebrate with people you love and care about. Listen. Learn. Love. Focus on what you know makes you feel good, and what makes you feel certain. Focus on your gifts. Focus on your gratitude.

And don't wait for Thanksgiving! Watching how much people enjoyed the occasion led me to start a new tradition: The Sunday Dinner. Every Sunday, I invite people to my table—to gather, to eat, to laugh. It's a tradition my kids have come to love and I've come to count on. Food, family, love, and laughter. Who says we have to do it only once a year?

Dear God, thank you for the experience of finding delight in even the simplest things in life. Help me never to take what you've given me for granted. Thank you, thank you, thank you. Amen.

What I'm Carrying with Me into Each New Year

"I keep turning over new leaves, and spoiling them, as I used to spoil my copy-books; and I make so many beginnings there never will be an end."

—**Laurie, in** Little Women
by Louisa May Alcott

The first few days of a brand-new year are thrilling. We have a chance to make the coming year our best one yet—personally, professionally, and politically.

Last New Year's, as I wrote down all the things I want to bury, burn, or just stop bitching about in the year ahead, I also made a list of all of the positive things in my life I wanted to carry into the new year. Making both lists is a useful practice I call "Bury and Bring."

Here are this year's Bury and Bring lists:

What I Want to Bury in the New Year

That critical voice in my head. It's so judgmental, so inaccurate, so boring. I want to blow it out and bury it once and for all.

My fear. I want to grab my fear by the you-know-what. It's got no place in my life in this coming year. Time is running short, but fear keeps me running in place. I'm burying it.

Comparisons. Even though I know that absolutely nothing good comes from making comparisons, I'm still making them, still comparing myself to someone else—my work to someone else's, my accomplishments to someone else's, my looks to someone else's, my relationships to someone else's, and on and on. Enough. No more.

Control. I'm also letting this go. It doesn't work anyway. I can't control what people think, say, or do, so I'm getting out of that ridiculous business.

What I Want to Bring into the New Year

My gratitude practice. Every morning, I thank God for my faith, my family, my friends, and my health. I want to keep doing that.

My meditation practice. I want to get better at this, because it makes me better at life.

My mental and physical health. I want to really make them a priority by really setting aside time for both. They go together, and they both deserve regular attention and practice.

My mission. I want to be bolder with my mission each year. My own personal mission is to play a role in getting to the bottom of this mystery surrounding Alzheimer's disease: that two-thirds of all brains diagnosed with Alzheimer's belong to women. That's terrifying and unacceptable. I know I need help doing this, so I'm going to bury my ego and keep reaching out to ask for help, even when I'm told to go away. Staying at this mission could help millions of families.

My voice. I also want to be bolder with my voice. I'm a journalist, but I'm also a citizen of this great country. I want to hear more positive, uplifting messages that can move us forward. Not just some of us. Not just women. Not just people of one color. All of us.

Each new year is a new chance for all of us to use our voices for good—challenging what is, imagining what can be, and moving ourselves, and humanity, forward.

Dear God, living with regret and guilt for my past mistakes is a heavy burden to carry. Free me from the chains of remorse over things I've done that I wish I could do over. Please help me know in my heart that I can make a fresh start whenever I decide to. Free me to look ahead and not keep looking back. Amen.

Don't Call Me an Empty Nester

All the art of living lies in a
fine mingling of letting go and
holding on.

—**Havelock Ellis**

When my youngest child, Christopher, graduated from high school, I thought about the idea of letting go. I told myself I was ready because he was ready. Boy, was I wrong.

I wasn't ready to really let go. I wasn't ready for the flood of emotions. I wasn't ready for the loss. And I really wasn't ready for all the questions I got from those around me.

"So, now what?" (**Uh . . .**)

"What are you going to do with all of that free time of yours?" (**Free time? What's free time?**)

"What are you going to do every night when you used to eat dinner with him?" **(I don't know? Learn to dance?)**

"What are you going to do with his room?" **(Why? Isn't he coming home for Christmas?)**

"What are you going to do with his dog?" **(Sleep with him myself.)**

"What are you going to do with yourself?" **(Do I have to do something with myself?)**

Facebook friends gave me sturdy advice:

"It's your turn now. Take time for yourself," said Sandy.

"Stay busy. Help others," said Kate.

"Wear sunglasses as you say your goodbyes," said Connie.

"Give yourself a two-week adjustment period," said Val.

"Give yourself six months. You will love it," said Lynne.

So when the moment came, I took a deep breath, moved my baby (oh, excuse me, "my young man") into the dorm, and moved myself out.

It helped that I could see how happy Christopher was. It helped that he told me, "Mom, you did a great job. Don't worry. I'm fine."

It helped that I knew I gave him my best and that he brought out a kinder, gentler me, which I'm rather enjoying. It also helped that after we finished moving him into his dorm, there was a football game I didn't have tickets to, so I was more or less forced to head out and back to my own life.

So, now what?

Well, I'm going to give myself the two weeks that were suggested (maybe I'll even allow myself the six months). I'm going to schedule dinners with friends who I haven't gone out with in, like, twenty-seven years! I'm going to keep my Sunday family dinners going, but I'm going to keep broadening the definition of family.

I'm also going to throw out any old "Mom clothes" still hanging in my closet for some weird reason. I'm going to look for adventures in every part of my life. I'm going to focus on my mission to find a cure for Alzheimer's, and I'm going to empower my heart and soul.

Look at that. I've got stuff to do! And that was the first day.

So on this blessed day when Mother Teresa of Calcutta is being canonized, I'm going to focus my motherly love on my other adult kids who still live in town, and I'm going to mother myself and anyone else who shows up looking for some motherly love. Mother Teresa's life has taught me to have faith, to stay in it and stay at it, to be of service, and to never, ever doubt the power—actually the miracle—of motherly love.

Understanding   motherly   love   makes

me realize that the empty-nest label is a misnomer—or better yet, an outdated label. Because once a mother, always a mother. A loving home is always a loving home (whether kids are in the nest or not).

I returned home from moving my son into his dorm with a heavy heart, and—I'm not going to lie—stirred up some fear and anxiety about how I was going to manage moving forward. But then I sat down, called up some of the intestinal fortitude my mother always talked about, and told myself this: There is nothing empty about my nest, my home, me, or my life! Dinner anyone?

· · ·

UPDATE: Well, the nest wasn't empty for long. First my older son graduated from college and moved back home with me. Then one of my East Coast nieces moved in to finish her senior year at a West Coast college.

When I took Christopher back for his sophomore year, I helped him move into a fraternity house, where he's living with twenty-four other young men. Yes, twenty-four. Sometimes I think he knows me better than I know myself, because when we hugged goodbye, he said, "Mom, I'm fine. It's all good!"

I know he's actually more than fine. He loves his college. He loves the decision he made to go there. He loves his band of brothers. And he loves his life. There's no better feeling than seeing someone you love so very happy.

And now as I write this, my older son and my niece are getting ready to move back out. Empty nest, here I come!

Dear God, thank you for the good friends you have brought into my children's lives. I ask yo to bless their relationships and pray that a sincere and genuine love may safeguard their hearts. Help me to love their friends and to bring them into the circle of our family. May my life be a blessing to them, as they are a blessing to me. Amen.

Sixty Life Lessons for My Birthday

> "As we let our own light shine, we unconsciously give other people permission to do the same. As we are liberated from our own fear, our presence automatically liberates others."
>
> **—Marianne Williamson**

I've been thinking about birthdays—especially my own! In our family, birthdays are a big deal. There are always balloons, cards, gifts, a homemade cake (my kids are the ones who know how to bake)—always a fun celebration of the gift of love, laughter, and life.

I love any excuse to have a party, but it's always a bit hard for me to celebrate my own birthday. That pushes me outside my comfort zone. Now, with the encouragement of my friends and family, I'm changing that. I'm allowing myself to be celebrated—though even writing that still feels weird! I'll say it again: **I'm allowing myself to be celebrated**.

As I stand on the cusp of a new decade, I'm focusing on all the gifts I've been given in my life and all the lessons I've learned. I'm happy to say I look forward to the next frontier, even though I admit I don't really have a master plan for what that entails.

But that doesn't matter, because plans are just that, plans, and life has a way of interrupting them. Friends and family die without warning. People you count on don't come through. You can end up disappointing yourself and others. But then again, total strangers can also show up and guide you to places you would never have imagined. Life is indeed a magical mystery tour!

So in honor of my own sixtieth birthday,

here are sixty life lessons I've learned along the way. I shared some of them with my kids, whereupon they burst into tears and asked me if I was dying. (Lordy!)

Now I share them with you, hoping they may help you on your own journey to live more authentically and to live more of your life without judgment of yourself or others. The goal is that when the time does come for you to go, you'll have fewer regrets about what you didn't do and more pride in what you did. Here goes:

1. There is nothing about life that's predictable, so stop trying to predict it.
2. Find every excuse you can to celebrate it.
3. Stop wishing you were a different age. Love the age you are.
4. Stop worrying about what others think. It's a huge waste of your time.
5. Stop wondering if God is listening. Just have faith he is.

6. Be grateful to anyone who has ever loved you or tried to love you.

7. Know that bad stuff happens in life. You think you won't be able to withstand it, but you can and you will. Just as you have before.

8. Be kind to your body, because it will be with you for life.

9. Trust me when I tell you this: Diets are a waste of time. I've tried them all.

10. Don't believe people who tell you they can eat anything and still be that skinny. They're lying!

11. Moderation in everything but laughter.

12. Don't be scared to be a parent. Trust your heart.

13. Make friends with your children's friends. They'll make you laugh and give you valuable intel.

14. Keep a pair of clothes from high school. Not to check if you can still fit in them, but for the memories they hold.

15. Hold your children over and over again, and then let someone hold you.
16. Get smart about money as early as possible.
17. Save something from every paycheck.
18. Buy comfortable sheets, because you'll spend a lot of time on them.
19. Know that no matter how smart you are, you can't change someone else.
20. Stay out of other people's business. Dealing with your own is a full-time job.
21. Be kind, because everyone else is struggling, too.
22. Don't engage in gossip. It always comes back and bites you in the butt.
23. Don't mistake gifts for love.
24. Stay connected with your childhood friends and introduce them to your grown-up friends. Make yours a generous tribe that's connected not only to you, but to one another.
25. Spend time alone when you're young, so

being alone won't scare you when you're older.

26. Write thank-you notes to people for their time and their wisdom. Regard both of those as gifts they've given you.

27. Look people in the eye when you talk to them. And at least once, look into someone's eyes for five minutes straight. You'll learn something.

28. Sit down to family dinner every night. If you can't do it every night, pick a night and make that a can't-miss-it Family Night.

29. Play games with your kids. (My favorites are Capture the Flag and Uno.)

30. Give your children a Get-Out-of-School Pass to use for a special day with you.

31. Keep an open table and an open mind.

32. Be of service.

33. Travel with your kids. It will broaden their horizons and strengthen your bonds.

34. Don't assume anyone is better than you or you are better than anyone else.

35. Don't ever sit out an election. Living in a country where every vote counts is a gift. Use yours.

36. Stay connected to your siblings, and don't come between them and their partners. My four brothers are my past, my present, and my future—and I love their wives.

37. It's a privilege to take care of your parents when they're aging and ailing.

38. Learn how to turn off the critical voice in your head as early and often as possible.

39. Every year write down your regrets, then burn them and leave the ashes where they belong: in the garbage.

40. Listen to your gut. It knows more than anyone you're asking for advice.

41. Practice prayer and meditation. It will keep you in contact with yourself.

42. Never think your work life is more important than your family.

43. Don't think bad stuff won't happen to you. Learn how to push through. Head up, shoulders back, keep on trudging.

44. Don't allow anyone to shame you. If you don't let them, they can't.

45. Get good at forgiveness. You'll need to practice it throughout your life.

46. Know that forgiving doesn't mean going back to what was. It means going forward with love. You get to decide what that looks like.

47. If you want forgiveness, ask for it.

48. Get good at letting go.

49. Don't expect people to be perfect. Just as you aren't, neither are they.

50. Learn how to communicate in your own home. If you can't find your voice, get help.

51. And don't think that reaching out for

help (see number 50) is a sign of weakness. It's a sign of strength.

52. Therapy isn't a waste of time. It can save a friendship, a marriage, your life.

53. If you marry and it comes to an end, don't let anyone tell you that you've failed—and don't tell that to yourself, either. Be grateful for the love you had, the memories you made, the lessons you learned.

54. If you do have a self-pity party, make it short, and then move on.

55. Don't see yourself as a victim. See yourself as brave.

56. Be brave enough to write your own story—and then rewrite it.

57. Be brave enough to try love after your heart has been broken.

58. Spend time in nature. It calms the mind.

59. Spend time with people who see you, celebrate you, and want the best for you.

60. Have faith that your best days are ahead of you, that your next frontier will be the

most fulfilling time of your life, and that you deserve to be seen as good enough just the way you are—including by yourself.

Whew.

Dear God, thank you for this life, my life. Thank you for my belief that the best is yet to come. Amen.

Hope

"They say a person needs just three things to be truly happy in this world: someone to love, something to do, and something to hope for."
—Tom Bodett

To keep going you must have hope. All of us have those days when we feel as though we can't go forward and can't go backward. We're just stuck.

When I feel that way, I reach into my back pocket and take out some hope.

That's right, I've always had hope. Hope that it would get better, hope that there was something wonderful around the corner, hope for my children, hope for my friends, hope for the world, and, yes, hope for me. I just have to remember to pull it out.

So sometimes when I can't catch my breath, I close my eyes and imagine myself out in what I call The Open Field. For me, The Open Field is a place of joy and laughter and community. It's a place where purpose-driven people gather to dream and collaborate and make their lives and their world better. It's a place of hope.

Right now, The Open Field is just an idea, but I'm hopeful that it won't always exists only in my own imagination. I hope we can find that common ground—a real place where we come together, where people of different generations and different belief systems coexist, care for one another, and care for our common home.

I keep hoping, and my hope keeps me going. Going forward with hope gives my life meaning.

When all else seems to fail, when you can't think of one more thing or do one more thing, when the solution seems to be escap-

ing you—reach into your own back pocket.
Pull out some hope. And with hope in your
heart, move forward into your own Open
Field.

> **Dear God,** please help me to not lose
> hope. Hope helps me to move forward.
> Please help me to maintain my hope in
> myself, in my neighbors, in humanity.
> Please help me to keep my hope alive.
> With hope in my heart, I believe that my
> best years are in front of me. I pray that it
> is so. Amen.

Epilogue

Who am I?
Why am I here?
What is my purpose?

Three questions
Three profound probing questions
Can you answer them?

If so, you are blessed
and you are probably already living a
beautiful meaningful life
If you are not there yet, don't give up hope
Just keep coming back to those three
questions

Who am I?
Why am I here?
What is my purpose?

Because who you are is unique
Why you are here is specific to you
And so is your purpose

Don't tell me you don't have a purpose
Don't think that there is nothing special
about you
Don't believe that mission and purpose
belong only to others
They are there for each of us

It is your destiny to live a beautiful
meaningful life
I have no doubt
It's why you are here

You are not here to be someone's echo
Someone's appendage
Someone's victim
You are here to fulfill your calling and your
mission

So
Keep your eyes open
keep your mind open
keep your heart open
Meaning is everywhere
Just like love
It's up to each of us to find it

Keep searching
keep thinking
keep writing
keep dreaming
keep getting up when life knocks you down
keep trying
keep fighting
keep laughing
keep loving

Imagine yourself at the end of your life
standing in an Open Field

How do you feel
Who is there with you

Did you figure out the answer to those first
three questions?
Of course you did.

Keep those answers in the forefront of your
mind
Keep moving forward toward that vision
It's yours to make a reality

You've got this
Yes you do
I'm so happy for you

###

Oh! And One More Thing: The Power of Reevaluating

"There comes a time in all of our lives when it's time to take stock of what was, what is, and what can be. Don't hold on to stuff that prevents you from becoming who you can be."
—Maria

I've been thinking it's time for me to take stock and reevaluate.

I usually do some kind of self-inventory around New Year's, but I can't wait until then. I just can't.

Why? Because my heart has called me out. Because my body has been yelling at me to pay attention. Because my mind is telling me to stop holding on to beliefs formed decades ago that no longer hold up or serve—beliefs that are banging around so hard in my head, they've been giving me migraine headaches, complete with a side order of what they call "vertigo and vestibular damage." Don't ask!

It wasn't just one thing that brought me to this moment. It's been a series of whispers—and then a few two-by-fours banging me over the head. If I've learned anything in life it's to pay attention to the whispers and the two-by-fours, because they usually precede a knockout.

Yes, what's been making me feel out of sync and out of step are beliefs formed long ago that just don't work for me anymore, but still I hold on to them.

They make me feel bad: burdened, self-righteous, judgmental. And guess what? I don't want to feel any of those things anymore—because as my mother would say, "They make you unattractive." And as I've experienced lately, being unattractive isn't the worst of it.

So, let's go. Here are a few things I wish I'd known sooner, but the only way I could have known them is to have gone through exactly what I've gone through.

Work

I used to be so judgmental of people who weren't working like maniacs. I was wrong. Working like a maniac only makes you a maniac. It can be its own addiction. It makes you sick. Put work in its proper place. Don't make it your life.

Politics

I used to think the Democratic Party had all the answers. I was wrong. Both parties contribute to the divisiveness in this country. Both parties have brought our civic discourse to this nasty and mean-spirited place. I left the Democratic Party a few years ago to register as an Independent. Therein lies my hope.

Catholicism

I used to think the Catholic Church had all the answers, but then I woke up. I vividly remember the overwhelming fear I felt the first time I missed Sunday mass. I thought I'd be going straight to hell for that infraction—but lo and behold, I didn't. Then when nothing bad happened either the first time I ate meat on Friday instead of fish, I began to realize that the Church wasn't all-knowing. Yes, I love Pope Francis and I love the nuns. I love the Sermon on the Mount and the Church's social justice platform. But I can't stand its positions on women, gays, sin, divorce, birth control, death with dignity—or the way they've handled the numerous cases of sex abuse by priests. Even with all that,

I still find comfort in going to church and being in conversation with what I know is a loving and forgiving God. And I still consider myself a good Catholic.

Men

I grew up in a family where there was lots of testosterone. I thought that's what it meant to be a man. I was wrong.

Kindness

I thought kindness was weakness. God, was I wrong. Now it's my most sought-after attribute in a friend.

Sex

I didn't grow up talking about sex, only about Mary Magdalene—and any Catholic girl my age knows what the Church thought of Mary Magdalene. When it came to sex, it was about guilt and shame.

But as a mother, I do talk openly to my kids about sex. I want my daughters to feel good about their sexuality, not guilty or ashamed. I want my sons to view it as a sacred act with someone you love, not an act of control over someone you're trying to "have." I want my kids to have a positive relationship with their sexuality—and never to judge someone whose sexuality is different from theirs.

Journalism

I used to think everyone involved in journalism was motivated by the truth, believed in facts, and wanted to do good with their work. I was wrong.

There's a lot of great journalism out there

and a lot of great and noble people doing the work, but like everything, it's imperfect.

Dividing all of it into "real" versus "fake" performs a disservice to all of us.

We are fortunate to live in a country with a free press, and we should never underestimate that right. But take it upon yourself to be informed about what's factual and what's not.

Addiction

When I was growing up, there were several people in my family struggling with drugs. I asked myself, why don't they just stop? I didn't understand addiction and how hard it is to get clean and stay that way. I had zero understanding of the hole people can have in their guts until I confronted my own. Everyone has a different way to fill that hole and deal with their pain and their fears.

I've learned that addiction isn't just about will. It often isn't enough to just want to stop. It's a disease. Those battling it need our support, our help, our compassion, and our respect for their bravery. I see this every day.

Therapy

Boy, was I wrong about this. I thought therapy was for people who were mentally ill, had lost either a parent or a child, or were suicidal. I was wrong.

I am a beneficiary of therapy. It's helped me tremendously to navigate the rough patches in my life, to be more aware, to forgive, and to be a better person. I recommend it sooner rather than later.

Health

I thought I could eat whatever I wanted for however long I wanted. Whoa, was I was wrong.

Bad choices catch up to you, and before you know it, you can find yourself backed into a corner, unable to get out. Or you could be the person whose bad choices make it easier for cancer to knock you out or Alzheimer's to take over. Please make your health a priority sooner than I did.

And while you're at it, get to the bottom of your relationship with food.

Surprise! Cookies aren't a substitute for real love. They don't love you back. Neither do cake, candy—and especially not Swedish fish, which I've "researched" extensively.

Get rest, both physical and mental. When I was growing up, rest was a big no-no. My parents never rested, so neither did my brothers nor I. Today I know better.

Rest isn't laziness. It's critical to your mental and physical well-being. It's recharging your mental and physical batteries, so you can forge ahead on all cylinders.

Motherhood

I can't even begin to describe how ill-informed I was about motherhood. I didn't know anything about the power and importance of attachment. I didn't have a clue. Nor did I have a clue how hard parenting is and how rewarding it can be. How I wish I could thank my mother in person today for her stamina as a mother of five.

Fear

I used to view myself as fearless because I skied the black diamond runs, jumped off cliffs, spoke up, and spoke out. Fear was a dirty word. Admitting it was even worse than having it.

But then I came face-to-face with how much fear I actually held in my body, as well as my mind. I came to recognize how fear had and continued to paralyze me in parts of my life.

Today I work hard at acknowledging my fear, feeling it, pushing through things that scare me emotionally—such as being vulnerable enough to share this list and admitting that I've been wrong about many things, admitting I'm often scared and feel alone.

Speaking of being alone: Very few things scare me more than being alone. In order not to be alone, I'd always packed my life and my house full of people, lots of people. That was in part because I was afraid not just to be alone, but also to even **look** like I was alone. Being alone for just one minute felt like I had always been alone and was doomed to be alone on this earth forever.

Well, well, well, look at me now! These days—with no more marriage and four children grown and gone—I spend quite a bit of time alone.

I'm not saying I love it yet, but I've learned most of the truths I'm sharing today because I've spent time alone—time in silence, time reevaluating myself and my beliefs. I'm getting more comfortable with it.

Marriage

I always thought people whose marriages didn't work out were quitters. I was wrong.

I do admire people who work in and at their marriages, but I also admire those who chart a new way forward. And I really admire those who manage to stay friends after their marriages are over—and aren't afraid to try love again after being hurt.

Divorce

I grew up thinking divorce was a sin.
  I couldn't have been more wrong.

Success

Big misjudgments here. I thought if I anchored a network news show, I'd feel successful. I thought if I won those big national journalism awards, I'd be a great success. I believed if I publish a bestselling book, I'd feel like I nailed it. And the list goes on. Do this, achieve that, and you'll feel like a sparklingly successful human being.

I was wrong. Success, I've learned, is an inside job. Believe me, I didn't grow up with that message.

The people whom I regard as the most successful aren't the ones I used to think were successful. Instead they are the ones who love and are loved. They are the ones who have beautiful, loving families. They are the ones who toil quietly and patiently on the frontlines of life.

(I wrote this before I saw that a napkin on which Albert Einstein had scribbled, **"A calm and modest life brings more happiness than the pursuit of success combined with constant restlessness,"** sold for $1.3 million at auction.)

Perfectionism

I thought perfection was attainable—by me, no less.

It's impossible because at first you feel empowered and brilliant for chasing the illusion that you can achieve perfection. But in the end you're doomed to feel ashamed because perfection just that: an unattainable illusion.

Coming face-to-face with my own imperfection, acknowledging my flaws, and accepting myself the way I am—right here and right now—has allowed me to embrace a kinder gentler more loving me.

Boundaries

I had never heard the word "boundaries" applied to human relations until I was in my fifties. Someone suggested I might have trouble establishing and honoring my own boundaries, and I had to ask what they meant. Now I know—and now I have them.

Privacy

We are all entitled to privacy, and you should fight for yours—especially now in this over-sharing world we live in.

Protect your privacy, protect your children's privacy. Put up boundaries and limits. Teach them there's no need to share everything. And that goes for us, too. Share a little if it can help others and keep the rest to yourself. It will be better for you, your relationships, and your children.

And oh, yes: Public people are entitled to privacy, too.

Loyalty

I grew up in a family where loyalty was king. I heard about it all the time: loyalty to family, loyalty to friends, loyalty to a particular faith, political party, or person. But it didn't dawn on me that any of these could crush loyalty to your own self. I never ever heard about loyalty to oneself.

Today loyalty to myself is more important than my loyalty to anyone or anything else. I've learned it's not selfish to put yourself at the center of your own life. I've learned that you must honor and be loyal to that person looking back at you in the mirror. The cost of not doing so is too high.

Love

I was so unclear about love, I'm not exactly even sure how to begin.

Let's just say I had it all wrong. Today I have an entirely different take on what love is.

I honor the small acts of love all around me that I used to not even allow into my consciousness: When someone brings me a coffee, opens the door for me, takes a walk with me, sits with me, listens to me, drives me to the doctor's, waits for me. Looks at me in a way that lets me know they're looking at me, not my name, my family, my job title. That's love, plain and simple.

Bottom Line: Reevaluate!

Reevaluating your life—whether it's on New Year's or your birthday or while you're sitting in the hospital with a sick friend—can be painful with regret and coulda-woulda-shoulda. But it can also be incredibly liberating.

Even though I've been wrong about a lot of things in my life, reevaluation has taught me I've also been right about a lot. Right about the importance of family. Right about certain friends. Right about my faith in a God larger than me or any one person or edifice.

And right that there was something in me worth fighting for.

Now we know that for sure, it's something we'll never have to reevaluate.

Dear God, please guide me forward in my life. Help me let go of beliefs and opinions that no longer serve me. Help me to drop critical judgments of myself and others. Remind me that I don't know other people's paths or pains. Help me to continue to grow into a more compassionate and caring human being—to others and to myself. Amen.

Acknowledgments

This little book is a gift from me to you—an offering of my thoughts, hopes, dreams, and prayers. As always, it wouldn't have been possible without the generous support, love, and guidance of these people:

I'm deeply grateful to Jan Miller and Shannon Marven, who have been my partners on every one of my books and who encouraged me to bring this one to life; to editor Pam Dorman, whose patience and expertise made my manuscript so much better; to Nayon Cho, who worked with me on the jacket; to my children Katherine, Christina, Patrick, and Christopher who taught me many of the lessons I've talked about in this book; to my friends Nadine, Erin, Patti,

Lindsay, Kelsey, and Margo who all gave spectacular feedback.

And most of all, thank you to my friend Roberta, who doesn't want to be acknowledged here, but who helped me become the writer I am, and whom I've loved working with all my life, even though anybody listening to us would swear that we were about to kill each other.